# The Economics
# of Efficiency
# and Growth

# The Economics of Efficiency and Growth

## Lessons From Israel and the West Bank

**Abba Lerner**
*Visiting distinguished Professor of Economics*
Queens College, University of New York
Member of the National Academy of Sciences

**Haim Ben–Shahar**
*Professor of Economics*
University of Tel Aviv, Israel

**Ballinger Publishing Company** ● Cambridge, Mass.
*A Subsidiary of J.B. Lippincott Company*

International Standard Book Number: 0–88410–276–9

Library of Congress Catalog Card Number: 74–32140

Printed in the United States of America


**Library of Congress Cataloging in Publication Data**

Lerner, Abba Ptachya, 1903–
   Economic policy in Israel.

   Based on the authors' Kalkalah ye'ilah.
   1.  Israel—Economic policy.  I.  Ben-Shahar, Haim, joint author.
II.  Title.
HC497.P2L39            330.9'5694'05          74–32140
ISBN 0–88410–276–9

# Contents

# List of Tables

# Preface

The purpose of this book is to contribute to the better understanding of economic growth and development. It makes use of the experience of Israel in illustrating its points.

Part I (Chapters 1-10) deals with the general principles of efficient economic policy, and Part II (Chapters 11-25) discusses various aspects of Israeli economic policy on the basis of these principles. Among the subjects examined are economic growth, prices and control, wage policy, credit policy, investment, saving, taxation, foreign trade and foreign exchange, inflation, employment and income distribution. Consideration is also given to the economic effects of the 1973 war. Special attention is paid to the role of government in economic activity and to the Israeli experience with economic planning. The book includes (Chapters 23-25) a review of economic development in the West Bank and the Gaza Strip and economic policy in these territories since 1967.

Readers do not need any prior knowledge of either basic economic theory or of the economic development of Israel. The essential background material is provided as needed. The book, therefore, would also be of value to readers primarily interested in economic theory, with developments Israel serving to illustrate the practical application of the basic principles.

The book would not have been possible without the generous assistance of a variety of institutions and people.

We want to express our thanks to the Foerder Institute of Economic Research for the resources it put at our disposal; to the University of Tel Aviv; to the City University of New York and to Columbia University for their assistance at various stages of our labors; to Tamir Agmon, who helped in the field research and to Zvi Adar for his useful suggestions. We extend our special thanks to Jack Gallagher, who edited portions of the book and to Mordecai S. Chertoff who prepared it for the press. We would be remiss were we not to express our gratitude to colleagues who assisted all along the way with both advice and encouragement and contributed greatly to the book's clarity. Only for the flaws do we take full responsibility.

A.L. - New York
H.B.S. - Tel Aviv
January 14, 1975

# Introduction

This volume is an outgrowth of the authors' Hebrew study (*Kalkala Ye'ila—The Efficient Economy* (Amikam, Jerusalem, Israel, 1969), a critical review of the achievements and failures of Israel's economic policy in the light of modern economic understanding. The study had been stimulated by the failure of the government to make the best use of the market mechanism for economic efficiency, progress and growth, and in particular by the government's attempt to check inflation and to improve the balance of trade by "slowing down" the economy. Inevitably *mitun,* the Hebrew word for this slowing down, came to mean recession.

We were very pleased with the reception of the study in Israel, all the more so because of the influence it seems to have had on economic policy. It seemed to us that with revision and enrichment by examples from Israel, it could have wider applicability. After all, the economic principles, set forth and illustrated here, are by nature of universal import.

In ancient times the land of Israel was a source of religious enlightenment. In modern times, and on quite a different field—that of economic performance—Israel has shown a 10.5 percent per annum average GNP growth rate, 6 percent percent per capita per annum for a *fourfold* increase in population during her first 25 years, which included three wars and a recession. The territories occupied since the 1967 war have enjoyed an even higher rate of economic progress. This achievement has led many, especially among the developing countries, to wonder whether they could not benefit from Israel's experience. This is the main question this book tries to answer.

There emerges, however, no clear "Go thou and do likewise." The greater part of Israel's economic success must be attributed to causes other than her economic policy. Indeed, that success was achieved in considerable measure despite her economic policy. Nevertheless, much can be learned even from errors, of both commission and omission, particularly in Israel, which has been seen as a "pressure cooker" or "test tube" for economic experiment.

Israel is a small country with negligible natural resources, which has had to devote an outstanding portion of its GNP to defense (25 percent in 1970; 40 percent in 1974). If its economic growth had been 5 percent instead of 10.5 percent per year, the total GNP would not have covered the 1974 defense expenditure. On the other hand, if Israel's economic growth continues at 10.5 percent, the 1974 absolute level of defense expenditure will be only 15 percent in ten years. Furthermore if, in spite of this and her extraordinary rate of immigration, Israel has been able to make such progress, what could she have done had she not had to contend with these special difficulties?

The sobering fact is that the government's economic policies *hampered* Israel's economic growth. To distinguish between the policies that helped and those that hindered, it is necessary to grasp the underlying principles of economic efficiency and the function of the price mechanism.

This is why the greater part of this book is not about growth at all but about economic efficiency. We are aware that this might seem reminiscent of Washington Irving's *Knickerbocker's History of New York,* which begins with theories about the creation of the world, on the grounds that if the world had not been created there would have been no New York. Why, then, another book on the theory of economic efficiency, rather than on economic growth? Why use Israel as a model?

The answer to the second question is that the example of Israel, misinterpreted, has a great potential to mislead. The answer to the first question, by far the more important, is that what is of practical import in the theory of growth is really nothing but the theory of economic efficiency. Growth must come either from increased efficiency or from increased investment; increased investment comes only from increased foreign aid or from increased savings— i.e., reduced consumption. Few countries can hope for as much foreign aid per capita as Israel has received and, in any case, increasing foreign aid is more a matter of politics than economics.

The degree to which consumption can be reduced is limited the more "developing" (i.e., the poorer) the country. For all countries the possibilities of getting increased investment out of improved efficiency much outrun the possibilities of reducing consumption, and Israel has special difficulties in reducing consumption because of her especially heavy burdens of immigration and defense. There is some truth in the claim often made (for ideological reasons) that investment could be increased by a reduction of consumption by the capitalists out of income received in the form of profits. This could indeed help. But against the 10 or 15 percent of GNP, the maximum which could be taken out of profits and still leave the economy viable—and which can of course only be done once—improved efficiency can increase output available for investment manyfold, as it has done in the past. A larger provision for investment can come from increasing the *size* of the cake than from diverting a larger *proportion* of it. Increasing the size of the cake of course includes attention to technical progress, managerial skills and proper use of the price mechanism.

The two sources of growth are not independent of each other. As efficiency increases output increases, and it is then easier to save and invest more. Increased investment, by improving capital, increases output further. There are, of course, other relationships between investment and efficiency. But the main truth still holds: there is a far greater potential for progress in efficiency than in austerity.

Much attention has been focused on esoteric, theoretical, mathematical investigations, having to do with long-run implications of different rates of saving (or different attitudes toward saving). At the other extreme there have been studies on how specific historical, geographical, geological, demographic, cultural, sociological, educational and anthropological characteristics affect economic growth possibilities. But none of these studies has affected the validity of the proposition that the most promising source of progress, with very few exceptions, is increased efficiency.

This brings us to the rather nice distinction between progress and growth. Both refer to an increase in output *per capita* over time. The distinction has to do with the manner in which the increase is brought about. Progress is the result irrespective of the measures that bring it about. Progress may be increased by economic policy for integrating market and managerial methods for the greater efficiency of the economy as a whole, by greater managerial competence, by technical progress, by increased workers' skill or productive effort. Growth is sacrificing current progress brought about by consumption so as to release resources for accumulating productive capital for increasing future output. It includes investment in capital, whether physical capital goods or human skills and knowledge, for use in the future. Growth policy, in short, is concerned with that increase in future output which is brought about by present austerity.

With this philosophy in mind we begin the book by spelling out the general principles of economic efficiency and then go on to deal with their practical application in Israel. A final chapter summarizes what other countries can learn from Israel's experience.

# Part I

# Basic Principles of Economic Efficiency

# Chapter One

# Efficiency in Production

## WHAT IS ECONOMIC ACTIVITY?

Economic activity is the production and distribution of goods and services. It consists of converting inputs into outputs. Inputs are the raw materials and factors of production (land, capital and labor); outputs are the goods and services.

Since raw materials and the factors of production are limited in quantity, economic activity entails a choice of alternatives. The materials and factors used for producing an item could have been used to produce something else—that is, they are "scarce," and scarcity is the father of economic activity.

As technology advances it becomes possible to produce more from the same resources, but technology does not eliminate scarcity. The sum total of goods and services the economy can produce at any time is limited. Scarcity is what creates the "economic problems" of production, distribution and consumption.

Whatever differences of opinion there may be concerning economic problems, there is general agreement that we strive to obtain the maximum possible satisfaction and well-being from existing resources. This means that we always seek to achieve the *maximum output* from the available materials, gearing production to consumers' tastes and preferences. The more efficient we are, the higher will be the level of welfare.

Three kinds of efficiency are involved in economic activity: (1) efficiency in the use of inputs (*production*); (2) efficiency in the use of the outputs (*consumption*); and (3) efficiency in matching production to consumption (*integration*). Efficiency in production is attained when maximum output is realized from resources. Efficiency in consumption implies maximum total satisfaction from given outputs. Integrated economic efficiency is attained when the constellation of outputs matches personal preferences. Welfare depends on these three kinds of efficiency, and it is on these that economic policy must concentrate.

*3*

**Technical Efficiency**

Efficiency in production itself contains three elements: (1) technical efficiency; (2) managerial efficiency and economic efficiency.

Technical efficiency in production implies the maximum of a particular output produced with a given quantity of a particular factor; for example, the maximum possible output of potatoes grown on an acre of land, or the maximum possible output of milk from a cow. But technical efficiency does not take us very far. What good is it if Daisy yields a world record 30,000 quarts of milk a year if this requires such great quantities of food, labor and equipment that the cost per quart is very high? While one might be curious to know how much milk a cow can be made to yield, or eager for his animal to be the "queen of the cows," economic considerations are another matter.

Additional inputs in the form of treatment and care of a cow should increase her output, but the increase in output will not be in proportion to the increase in input. The increase in output from an added unit of input is called its marginal product. We shall see, in fact, that the marginal product will normally be diminishing. There will be smaller and smaller marginal products from equal additions to input.

This is, indeed, the general law of production. It is known as the law of diminishing marginal product. As we keep adding units of an input, a point will be reached when further inputs will yield no further output at all. The marginal product will have become zero. Additional inputs are only wasted.

But there will have been some waste even before this point is reached. The marginal product will have fallen very low, that is, the units of input with the very low marginal product could then be transferred to the production of other goods where their marginal product is not so low. Total output must then increase.

For example, instead of coddling nine cows, maximizing their output so as to bring them to championship levels, it is cheaper to keep ten cows, each of which produces 10 percent less milk. Total output will be the same, yet— by the law of diminishing marginal product—foregoing 10 percent of the yield from a cow which has been pushed to her peak output will save more than 10 percent of the inputs needed to bring her to this peak. Only a part of the input saved would be spent on the tenth cow, and the rest could be directed to additional milk production (say an eleventh cow), or to the production of other goods.

Note that we have done a remarkable thing. By altering the *allocation* of the unchanged supply of factors of production we have increased output! Thus, *technical efficiency* is not enough. *We can do better* if we take into account not only one of the factors of production (the cow), but all the other factors of production as well. Technical efficiency is sacrificed. We no longer get as much milk from each cow, but we get more output from the same inputs.

We shall see that in a closely corresponding manner we can improve on purely technical efficiency if we take into account not only one product (the milk) but also other products that can be produced with the same resources. This brings us to the concept of managerial efficiency.

### Managerial Efficiency

All economic activity consists of the conversion of inputs into outputs. The choice of inputs, outputs and methods for converting one into the other are called managerial decisions. Managerial efficiency differs from technical efficiency in that it considers not a single unit of input (the champion cow) and a single output (milk) but all the different kinds of input and all the different kinds of output in the firm.

Consider a farm of 100 acres of land with 100 workers. All the workers are equally skilled and all the land is equally good. Assume further that there are only two factors of production, land and labor, and that the only crop is potatoes. The workers must perform several tasks: seeding, watering, weeding and pruning. They will get the maximum yield from the land if the workers are so allocated that the marginal product of each worker is the same in each task. If the marginal product of a worker in seeding is 4500 pounds of potatoes, while in pruning it is 2500 pounds, the maximum yield is not being obtained. The manager is not efficient. He could increase the yield by shifting a worker from pruning to seeding, and realize an increase of 2000 pounds. Transferring more workers from pruning to seeding will further increase the output. But by virtue of the law of diminishing marginal product, transfers will decrease the marginal product of a worker in seeding below 4500 pounds and will raise that in pruning above 2500 pounds. The manager will get maximum output when the marginal products in pruning and seeding become equal.

This principle is applicable to every aspect of the production of every product. For maximum output the marginal product of each factor must be the same in every activity.

Assume that the farm also grows tomatoes. Having efficiently allocated the factors of production in growing potatoes, the manager of the farm must also allocate the tomato workers among the tasks so as to equalize their marginal products. Having done so, there is still the problem of allocating the factors of production between the two crops. If the manager were to assign half the land and half the workers to growing each crop, and if each factor's marginal product is the same in all tasks, the marginal products would be as follows:

|  | *One more worker* | *One more acre* |
|---|---|---|
| Tomatoes | 1000 pounds | 500 pounds |
| Potatoes | 4000 pounds | 600 pounds |

From this it can be seen that if a worker is added to any one task involved in growing tomatoes, the tomato output will increase by 1000 pounds. If a worker is added to growing potatoes, the potato output will be increased by 4000 pounds. On the other hand, if an acre is added to growing tomatoes, the output will be increased by 500 pounds; an additional acre allocated to potatoes will increase output by 600 pounds.

This allocation of the factors of production is not efficient. If we transfer one worker from tomatoes to potatoes, this reduces the output of tomatoes by 1000 pounds while it increases potato output by 4000 pounds. We can bring the tomato output back to its previous level by shifting 2 acres of land from potatoes to tomatoes. The reallocation of land does indeed reduce potato output by 1200 pounds, but we still have a net increase of 2800 pounds of potatoes. By changing the allocation of the factors of production, we increase the yield.

We can continue to increase output by shifting workers from tomatoes to potatoes, and land in the opposite direction. However, this procedure does not continue to be quite as beneficial. As the number of workers in tomatoes is decreased and the amount of land increased, the marginal product of tomato workers rises above 1000 pounds and the marginal product of tomato land falls below 500 pounds. At the same time, as the number of workers in potatoes is increased and the land decreased, the marginal product of potato workers falls below 4000 pounds, while the marginal product of the potato land rises above 600 pounds. When it is no longer possible to increase output by transferring workers and land, we have achieved maximum output; that is, we have managerial efficiency, as the following makes clear:

|  | *One more worker* | *One more acre* |
|---|---|---|
| Tomatoes | 1600 pounds | 400 pounds |
| Potatoes | 3600 pounds | 900 pounds |

For each worker that we shift from tomatoes to potatoes, we now have to shift 4 acres of land in the other direction to maintain the tomato output. The increase in potato yield from adding one worker (3600 pounds) is no longer greater than the reduction in output from removing the 4 acres. There is no gain from the shifting of the resources because we have the following equation:

$$\frac{1600}{400} = \frac{3600}{900}$$

That is,

$$\frac{\text{marginal product of tomato workers}}{\text{marginal yield of tomato land}} = \frac{\text{marginal product of potato workers}}{\text{marginal yield of potato land}}$$

This is the general condition for managerial efficiency in production: *the ratio of marginal products for any two factors must be the same in all the different products.*

Managerial efficiency is concerned with the single farm or firm. The economy as a whole is, however, composed of many farms or firms. Even if each is managed efficiently, we still have to ask whether the economy as a whole has achieved maximum output.

### Economic Efficiency

Economic efficiency in production is reached only when the whole economy obtains maximum output from its inputs. For economic efficiency in production we may need to shift factors from one firm to another.

Assume now that there are two farms, I and II, both producing potatoes and tomatoes. Both farms are managed efficiently, each achieving maximum output from its inputs. The marginal product for each factor on each farm is as follows:

|          | Farm I | | Farm II | |
|----------|--------|------|--------|-------|
|          | *Worker* | *Acres* | *Worker* | *Acres* |
| Tomatoes | 1600 | 400 | 1000 | 1200 |
| Potatoes | 3600 | 900 | 1500 | 1800 |

Here no reallocation of factors within the farm can increase output. The managers of the farms cannot be charged with inefficiency. All factors are employed most efficiently in each firm. But output can nevertheless be raised by transferring workers from one farm to the other. If we transfer a tomato worker from Farm II to Farm I, the total output of tomatoes will increase by 600 units without changing the output of potatoes. A similar transfer for potatoes increases output by 2100 units without affecting the output of tomatoes. Since it is possible to increase total output, there must be economic inefficiency. The inefficiency is not, however, due to inefficient allocation of factors within a farm but to inefficient allocation of the inputs between the two farms. The increase in output is possible because the marginal products, both of workers and of land, are different in the two farms.

If we transfer workers from Farm II to Farm I, in Farm I the marginal product of workers will decline (as the number of workers per acre increased), and the marginal product of land will rise (as the number of acres per 100 workers decreases). In Farm II, though, the marginal product of workers will rise and that of land will fall. There will thus be a narrowing of the differences between the marginal products in the two farms. Maximum output is obtained when these differences are reduced to zero; that is, when marginal products are the same on both farms. Thus:

|          | Farm I | | Farm II | |
| --- | --- | --- | --- | --- |
|          | Worker | Acres | Worker | Acres |
| Tomatoes | 1200 | 600 | 1200 | 600 |
| Potatoes | 3000 | 1500 | 3000 | 1500 |

Now that economic efficiency has been realized, 1 pound of tomatoes can be transformed into 2½ pounds of potatoes, not by magic but by shifting either factor in either farm from tomatoes to potatoes. The *marginal rate of transformation* of tomatoes into potatoes is 2½.

We may now formulate in more general terms the conditions for *economic efficiency* in production. If the allocation of the inputs is not efficient, it is possible to increase the output of one product without diminishing the output of any other product. Where it is efficient, no output (A) can be increased without reducing some other output (B). Such an unavoidable reduction of the output of B can then be considered an "input" which is transformed into the additional output of A. The reallocation of resources is then a "transformation" of B into A. In this way any reduction of an output (B) is considered an input in the production of the output that is increased (A).

Economic efficiency in production thus obtains when the *marginal rate of transformation of each kind of input into each kind of output is the same throughout the economy.*

Just as a reduction in the output of (B) permits an increase in (A), and the reduction can be considered an *input* in the production of more (A), so can a decrease in the output of (A) be considered an *input* in the production of (B). That reduction is precisely what an *efficient* economy has to suffer to be able to produce an additional unit of any product. This is the *marginal sacrifice* involved, or the *marginal cost* of any product in the deepest and ultimate sense. The marginal cost of any product is the *marginal alternative product,* what we could have had in place of the marginal output which we in fact do have. Thus, for example, the marginal cost, or the marginal alternative product, of 1 pound of tomatoes is 5/2 or 2½ pounds of potatoes, and the marginal cost, or the marginal alternative product, of a pound of potatoes is 2/5 of a pound of tomatoes. We can also say that the marginal rate of transformation between tomatoes and potatoes is 2:5 or 1:2½, or that the *marginal transformability* of tomatoes into potatoes is 2½, or that the marginal transformability of potatoes into tomatoes is 2/5 (= 1/2.5).

The economist is interested in the loss due to the lack of economic efficiency; he is generally not a specialist in managerial efficiency. The latter is a problem calling for the technical expertise of a manager, a type of specialization resembling that of an architect or a mechanic.

To obtain economic efficiency in production we need a suitable mechanism or system. When the marginal rates of transformation are unequal, the system must activate forces that will transfer inputs from firms in which the marginal transformabilities are lower, to firms in which they are higher. The system must also assure the continuation of this procedure until equality of the marginal rates of transformation is reached. In Chapters 4–9 we will discuss different systems for obtaining equality of the marginal rates of transformation. Before doing so, we will deal with some other problems of economic efficiency.

# Chapter Two

# Economic Efficiency in Consumption

In the previous chapter we considered economic efficiency in production, that is, how to attain maximum output from given inputs. There remains the problem of efficient distribution of the output among the consumers.

The purpose or function of a product is to provide satisfaction—enjoyment by individuals in its consumption. The satisfaction the consumer derives from a product is its utility. In general, the greater the consumption of a product the greater the utility. The additional utility provided by the addition of a unit of consumption is called the *marginal utility* of the product. But while the *total* utility increases with consumption, the *marginal utility* gets smaller and smaller. Thus the marginal utility of water, when it is in short supply and tightly rationed, is much greater than when it is plentiful. The marginal utility of an only shirt is greater than the marginal utility of that same shirt if it is one of ten shirts.

### Individual Efficiency

Assume that every consumer receives a fixed quantity of every product. His problem is how to get the greatest satisfaction from them. Continuing with the example of the previous chapter, suppose a consumer, Reuben, has at his disposal only two products, tomatoes and potatoes.

Tomatoes and potatoes can be used in various ways. Tomatoes, for example, can be eaten as they are, they can be used in salad, in soup, and so on. In order to get maximum satisfaction from the tomatoes, Reuben must divide them among the different uses so that the marginal utility of an additional pound is the same in every instance. As long as the marginal utility is greater in making salad than in making soup, Reuben can increase his total utility by transferring tomatoes from soup to salad. But as he does this the marginal utility of tomatoes used for salad will decrease while its marginal utility when used for soup will increase, until the difference in marginal utility disappears. This will establish the limit of total satisfaction that Reuben can obtain from his tomatoes. *The utility of a product is at a maximum when all its marginal utilities are equal.*

So it is also with the uses of Reuben's potatoes. When all the marginal utilities are the same, he has maximized his total utility from potatoes. Reuben will then have realized *individual efficiency* in consumption.

### Social Efficiency

Even if every consumer is individually efficient in consumption, all consumers together have not necessarily reached maximum utility. Such a maximum total utility is realized only when each product has the same marginal utility for *every* consumer.

If this equality does not obtain, it is possible to increase total utility by transferring tomatoes or potatoes from a consumer for whom they have a lower marginal utility to one for whom the marginal utility is higher. The gain from such a transference is the difference between the marginal utilities. Again, for the consumer who gets the additional tomatoes or potatoes, the marginal utility decreases. For the consumer whose supply has been reduced, the marginal utility increases. When the marginal utilities of both products become equal for all consumers, total utility has been maximized. It is no longer possible to increase total utility. The socially efficient distribution of products maximizes total utility.

### Economic Efficiency

This procedure cannot be carried out in practice simply because there is no way to measure marginal utility. Hence we cannot effect the equality of the marginal utilities. Even so, it is possible to improve the efficiency of distribution, and that can be done *without* measuring utilities. We can still get *economic efficiency* without equalizing the *marginal utilities* of different individuals by equalizing only the *marginal substitutabilities*.

Let us suppose that Reuben, after he became individually efficient in consuming his tomatoes and potatoes, is willing to give up 1 pound of tomatoes in return for 2 pounds of potatoes. This shows that for Reuben the marginal utility of 1 pound of tomatoes equals the marginal utility of 2 pounds of potatoes. He is *indifferent* as to 1 pound more of tomatoes or 2 pounds more of potatoes. His marginal substitutability of tomatoes for potatoes is 2. He is just willing to take 2 pounds of potatoes for 1 pound of tomatoes, that is, 1 pound of tomatoes is as good as, can substitute for, 2 pounds of potatoes. Conversely, his marginal substitutability of potatoes for tomatoes is 1/2.

Another consumer, Simon, has also reached individual efficiency in consumption, but has a different marginal substitutability. He is just willing to give up 1 pound of tomatoes for 3/4 pound of potatoes. The marginal utility of 1 pound of tomatoes is equal to the marginal utility of 3/4 pound of potatoes. His marginal substitutability of tomatoes for potatoes is 3/4, and that of potatoes for tomatoes is 4/3, or 1⅓.

In these conditions it is possible to increase the total utility of tomatoes and potatoes for Reuben and Simon by transferring tomatoes from Simon to Reuben and potatoes from Reuben to Simon. If Simon gives Reuben 1 pound of tomatoes and receives in exchange, say, 1¼ pounds of potatoes, Simon's condition improves. He would have been satisfied with 3/4 pounds of potatoes, but he received 1¼ pounds. Reuben's position also improves: He was willing to give up 2 pounds of potatoes for 1 pound of tomatoes, but he gave up only 1¼ pounds. Thus the utility of each consumer has increased, and so has the total utility.

It is worthwhile for Reuben and Simon to keep on exchanging as long as their marginal substitutabilities differ. But as the exchange continues, the tomatoes will yield Reuben a declining marginal utility, while the potatoes will yield an increasing marginal utility. Reuben will therefore be willing to give up fewer potatoes for a pound of tomatoes. Reuben's marginal substitutability of potatoes for tomatoes rises. He will no longer be satisfied with 1 pound of tomatoes for 2 pounds of potatoes. His marginal substitutability of potatoes for tomatoes will rise above 1/2 (and that of tomatoes for potatoes will fall below 2).

Corresponding changes take place for Simon, but in the opposite direction. His increased consumption of potatoes and decreased consumption of tomatoes will raise his marginal substitutability of tomatoes for potatoes above 3/4 (and that of potatoes for tomatoes will fall below 1⅓).

Thus the marginal substitutabilities of tomatoes for potatoes converge until they coincide somewhere between Reuben's 2 and Simon's 3/4. For example, the common marginal substitutability of tomatoes for potatoes, may be, say, 1½ (and the common marginal substitutability of potatoes for tomatoes 2/3). The marginal rate of substitution between potatoes and tomatoes is the same for Reuben and for Simon. When the marginal substitutabilities coincide, improvement is no longer possible and we have economic efficiency in consumption.

This principle of distribution can be applied to all products among all consumers. The general principle of economic efficiency in consumption is: *The marginal rate of substitution between every pair of products must be the same for all who consume them.*

But even if this principle is satisfied and we have attained an efficient distribution among the consumers, it is still not necessarily the best possible distribution. Something is still missing. It is true that it is no longer possible to improve the position of one consumer without worsening that of another. If we could compare the marginal utilities of different consumers, total utility could still be increased by transferring products in *only one direction*—from consumers with lower marginal utilities to those with higher marginal utilities. The consumer with the lower marginal utility would lose, but the gain to the other consumer would exceed his loss. We would be able to achieve social efficiency in consumption. But there is no way of comparing the marginal utilities of different consumers.

This raises another question, no less important: What division of *income* will maximize total utility? Since we lack any means of measuring utilities, we cannot answer this question. Nevertheless, the principle of diminishing marginal utility leads to the conclusion that, in general, the marginal utility of income is lower for a wealthy man than for a poor man. For this reason we can assume that, everything else being equal, a transfer of income from rich to poor, more equally distributing the same total income, increases total utility.

At any rate, changes in the division of income will cause changes in the marginal substitutabilities between products. Accordingly, if there is a new division of income, we will again be able to improve the distribution of products to restore economic efficiency in consumption. In this way we will once more improve the situation of every consumer.

For consumption, as for production, it is necessary to construct a system whereby an economically efficient distribution of the consumption of goods is assured. This will be treated in later chapters.

**Chapter Three**

# Integrated Efficiency in Production and Consumption

Economic efficiency in production is achieved when the marginal rate of transformation between every pair of products is the same for every producer, and there is economic efficiency in consumption when the marginal rate of substitution between every pair of products is the same for every consumer. When there is economic efficiency in production, it is impossible, without reducing the output of another product, to increase the output of any product by changing the allocation of inputs. When economic efficiency in consumption obtains, it is impossible, without worsening the situation of one consumer, to improve the situation of another individual by changes in the distribution of the output. However, even when there is economic efficiency in both production and consumption, we still cannot be certain that production corresponds to consumers needs—that the goods and services being produced are those that bring maximum satisfaction of all consumers. We may still be able to improve the situation by adjusting outputs to consumer preference. Such improvements are possible as long as for any pair of products the marginal rate of *transformation* (which is the same for every producer) differs from the marginal rate of *substitution* (which is the same for every consumer).

Let us return to tomatoes and potatoes. In Chapter 1, economic efficiency in production was realized when the marginal rate of transformation of tomatoes to potatoes was 2½. This means that by giving up 1 pound of tomatoes, resources were made available sufficient for growing an additional 2½ pounds of potatoes. In Chapter 2, economic efficiency in consumption was realized when the marginal rate of substitution of tomatoes for potatoes was 1½. Every consumer required 1½ pounds of potatoes to compensate him for giving up 1 pound of tomatoes. In summary,

|  | Marginal rate of transformation (in production) | Marginal rate of substitution (in consumption) |
|---|---|---|
| Tomatoes:Potatoes | 1:2½ | 1:1½ |

This table shows that we have not reached *integrated* economic efficiency. We can improve consumers' welfare if we can offer them, in return for 1 pound of tomatoes, anything more than 1½ pounds of potatoes. And indeed this can be done, because foregoing the production of 1 pound of tomatoes makes possible the production of 2½ pounds more of potatoes. We can transfer inputs of labor and of land from tomatoes to potatoes, continuing this procedure as long as there is a gap between the marginal transformability and the marginal substitutability. However, the gap will *narrow* because of the principle of increasing resistance here, in the form of diminishing marginal product and diminishing marginal utility.

As the output of potatoes rises, it becomes harder to produce them. The marginal product diminishes. And as the output of tomatoes is diminished, the law works in reverse—the marginal product increases. Tomatoes become easier to produce. Giving up a pound of tomatoes releases fewer resources, and these resources, furthermore, have a smaller marginal product in potatoes. Thus the marginal transformability of tomatoes into potatoes *diminishes,* and falls below 2½.

At the same time the increased consumption of potatoes reduces their marginal utility, while reduced consumption raises that of tomatoes. Consumers are now *less* willing to give up scarcer tomatoes for more plentiful potatoes. They will now require more than the 1½ pounds of potatoes in exchange. The marginal substitutability of tomatoes for potatoes rises above 1½.

The principle of increasing resistance thus operates from both ends. As the marginal transformability of tomatoes for potatoes falls below 2½ and the marginal substitutability of tomatoes for potatoes rises above 1½, the gap between the two diminishes. It disappears when the marginal transformability equals the marginal substitutability. We may assume that this will occur at 2, so that 1 pound of tomatoes and 2 pounds of potatoes are equivalent alternatives both in production and in consumption.

It is then no longer possible to improve the welfare of consumers by shifting production and consumption from one kind of goods to another. The economy now has reached *integrated economic efficiency* in production and consumption. Integrated economic efficiency is thus defined as *economic efficiency in production, economic efficiency in consumption, and efficient adjustment of production to consumer preferences.* Then the marginal rates of transformation between every pair of products is the same for every producer, the marginal rate of substitution between them is the same for every consumer, and the marginal rate of transformation is equal to the marginal rate of substitution.

If the economy is not in a state of integrated economic efficiency, the welfare of all or some consumers can be improved, without harming other consumers, by appropriate changes in production and consumption.

Among the products that contribute to well-being, in addition to clothing, food, cars and so on, we must include worker benefits and pleasant working conditions as important products whose marginal transformabilities and marginal substitutabilities must also be equalized for integrated economic efficiency.

# Chapter Four

# Economic Efficiency and the Price Mechanism

So far we have spelled out the conditions that must be met to achieve economic efficiency, but we have not considered how we can induce producers and consumers to behave so as to bring it about.

### Economic Efficiency in Consumption

Assume that we have at our disposal certain goods and services. The problem is to ensure economic efficiency in their consumption. For efficient distribution we must know the tastes and preferences of every individual. In a small group—such as a family—its head would be thoroughly familiar with the preferences of the members. Taking these preferences into consideration he could distribute the goods among them so as to raise the total utility to the maximum. He could equalize not only the marginal rates of substitution between any two products but also the marginal utilities of each product for the different members of the family. However, it is impossible to know their personal preferences in relation to every product. We must therefore find a technique that will serve in place of such knowledge. This is how it can be done.

Every consumer receives a sum of money on the first of the month to support him through the month. With this money he can buy as much as he wishes of every good and service. For every good and service there is a price which is the same for every consumer. Let us assume that the consumer must divide his expenditure between two products: tomatoes and potatoes. The price of potatoes is 50¢ per pound and that of tomatoes is $1 per pound. The consumer will spend his money so that the utility of an additional dollar's worth of tomatoes is equal to the utility of an additional dollar's worth of potatoes. He will then be indifferent to the shifting of a marginal dollar from tomatoes to potatoes, or the reverse.

Suppose the consumer spends his money so that the marginal utility of $1 worth of potatoes is less than that of $1 worth of tomatoes. The consumer will then not be indifferent. He will clearly gain from the shift by the excess of the marginal utility of $1 worth of tomatoes. He will therefore shift dollars this way as long as the difference in the marginal utility exists. When these marginal utilities become equal he will become indifferent between 2 pounds of potatoes and 1 pound of tomatoes. Now he can no longer improve his portion by shifting. He has reached his maximum utility by choosing a pattern of consumption in which the marginal rate of substitution between potatoes and tomatoes is equal to the ratio of their prices. This is how the consumer adjusts to the price structure.

The prices of potatoes and tomatoes being the same for every consumer, and every consumer adjusting his spending so that the marginal rate of substitution between potatoes and tomatoes equals the ratio between their prices, then the marginal rate of substitution will be the same for all consumers and the condition of economic efficiency in consumption is satisfied. If the consumers are free to spend their money over a wide range of goods and services whose prices are the same for everybody, this condition will be reached for every pair of products. Thus there is a method for equalizing the marginal rate of substitution between every two products bought by every consumer. An efficient distribution is realized automatically by consumers adjusting their consumption to a common set of prices—a price structure.

Here is seemingly a miraculous phenomenon. Nobody knows the personal preferences of anyone else—in any case, no one takes them into account. Each consumer considers only whether a dollar's worth of one item is as useful to him as a dollar's worth of anything else. In other words, he will consider whether 1 pound of tomatoes, which costs as much as 2 pounds of potatoes, has as much utility as 2 pounds of potatoes, and adjust his spending accordingly. In this manner a procedure is set in motion that automatically brings about economic efficiency in consumption.

There is, of course, nothing really miraculous about this phenomenon. The price of a product tells the consumer not only what he has to pay for another additional unit of it, but also what every other consumer has to pay; thus the prices indicate the relative marginal preferences of consumers for the product. If the relative preference of one consumer for a product is greater than that of other consumers, he will buy more of it: if his relative preference is lower than that of other consumers he will reduce his purchases. In either case he will increase or lower his expenditure on the different items until his relative preference is equal to the relative price, and thus also to the relative preference of everybody else. Only when his relative preferences equal those of the other consumers will his consumption neither increase nor decrease. Adjustments to the price structure, therefore, bring about an efficient distribution of consumption goods and services. But equality of the marginal rate of substitution between any two products for all consumers does not mean that the marginal utility of every product is the same for every consumer. That would require adjustments in the division of income, as we shall see in later chapters.

**Economic Efficiency in Production**

The price mechanism can serve to bring about not only economic efficiency in consumption but also economic efficiency in production, providing the managers of firms seeking the maximum possible profit allocate the factors of production according to the principles of efficient management. Firm A produces potatoes that sell for 50¢ a pound, and firm B produces tomatoes that sell for $1 a pound. Let us assume that the only inputs are land and labor. The wage of a worker is $1000 a year. As the number of workers increases for a firm the output is also increased; but beyond a certain point the marginal output of a worker diminishes.

To maximize its profit, firm A will increase the number of workers until the value of a worker's marginal output (in every activity) is equal to his wage. Thus if the marginal output per worker is greater than 2000 pounds of potatoes (say 3000) or 1000 pounds of tomatoes (say 1500), then the income from employing another worker is $1500 (i.e., $500 more than the wage). The manager then will add workers. If the marginal output of a worker is less than 2000 pounds of potatoes (or less than 1000 pounds of tomatoes), the marginal income will be less than the wage and the manager will reduce the number of workers. In every firm, therefore, the value of the marginal output of a worker will be made equal to the wage. More generally, the producer will increase or decrease the quantity he uses of every factor of production until the value of its marginal output is equal to its price.

When this condition obtains it will also be true that the marginal cost of producing a unit of any output will be equal to its price. The cost of producing an additional 2000 pounds of potatoes is the wage of an additional worker—$1000. This comes to 50¢ per pound, which is the price of the product. The same goes for every other product.

Economic efficiency in production requires the marginal rate of transformation between any two products to be the same for all producers. This condition will now be satisfied. For every firm producing potatoes the marginal cost is 50¢, while for every firm producing tomatoes the marginal cost is $1. Transferring a worker from potatoes to tomatoes will decrease potatoes by 2000 pounds, and increase tomatoes by 1000 pounds, and it makes no difference from what firm or to what firm he is transferred. The marginal transformabilities of labor into potatoes (2000) and of labor into tomatoes (1000) and of any factor into any product are the same throughout the economy. By virtue of the parallel between inputs and outputs pointed out in Chapter 1, a reduction in potatoe output is an input for tomatoes, and vice versa. Throughout the economy a sacrifice of 2 pounds of potatoes makes possible an increase of 1 pound of tomatoes, and vice versa. Accordingly, there obtains the condition for efficiency in production: equality of the marginal rate of transformation between every two alternative products throughout the economy.

Any firm that produces both potatoes and tomatoes can realize maximum profit only if its inputs are used so that the marginal expenditure in producing 2 pounds of potatoes equals that in producing 1 pound of tomatoes. If this is not the case the firm can transfer inputs to increase profits. The price structure is a guide to the efficient allocation of inputs among the different outputs. For managerial efficiency, the firm must base its decisions concerning inputs and outputs on the price structure.

In reality, production is extremely complicated. The inputs of one producer are the outputs of others; and these are the result of other inputs, in part the outputs of yet other producers, and so on. For example, potatoes require water and fertilizer, among other things. The water company has wells on which it employs pumps, fuel and manpower. The pumps come from other firms, the fuel from a refinery, which uses petroleum drawn from oil wells by other inputs. The petroleum is brought to the storage depots by tankers, which were themselves the product of thousands of different inputs. Watering the potato crop thus involves a vast and complex structure of inputs. Nevertheless, if there is an effective common price for every input and output, the producers will bring about the required equality between the marginal cost and the price of each output, and between the value of the marginal product and the price of each input.

It might seem that in order to achieve the efficient allocation of inputs and outputs one would have to know the structure of costs of production in every firm. If, indeed, we could know this, we could allocate inputs to each firm with detailed instructions for its operation. Economic efficiency in production would then be achieved entirely by the *management* method. While such knowledge is not available, the price mechanism does make economic efficiency of production possible, with each producer knowing only *his own* cost structure, and neither knowing nor caring about what other producers are doing. The prices each producer faces indicate the importance elsewhere of his outputs and his inputs, and that is all the information he really needs.

If the value of the marginal product of a factor of production is high for one producer relative to others, he will increase his use of the factor; if it is relatively low the producer will reduce its use. Only when the value of the marginal product of a factor is the same for this producer as for all other producers will he stop increasing or decreasing the factor's use in the manufacture of that product.

### Integrated Economic Efficiency

Integrated economic efficiency requires that for every pair of products the marginal rate of transformation (equalized for economic efficiency in production) and the marginal rate of substitution (equalized for economic efficiency in consumption) be equal to each other. This will come about automatically if only the producer's prices are the same as the consumer's prices.

We have thus seen how integrated economic efficiency can be attained by producers and consumers adjusting to the same price structure. But we still have not examined how the appropriate price structure is reached—the set of prices at which consumers and producers are able to buy and sell freely whatever quantities they may desire of every input and output. Every buyer needs a seller and vice versa. No quantity can be bought if it is not offered for sale; nothing can be sold if there is no buyer. Therefore the price must be such as to bring about equality between the quantity of each item demanded by buyers and the quantity offered by sellers.

A price that enables everyone to buy or sell as much as he desires is a genuine price. If people cannot buy or sell as much as they want to, then the prices are not genuine. If demand does not equal the supply of any item, the price must change until equality is achieved.

If purchasers want to buy more than what is for sale, the price is too low, and it must rise. As the price rises the quantity demanded will diminish, because some demand will be diverted to other products. At the same time, a rise in price will encourage production. Thus an increase in price reduces excess demand until there is equality between demand and supply. Similarly, an excess of supply over demand would be cured by a fall in the price. The mechanism for such raising and lowering of prices to equal supply and demand, and thus make the prices genuine, can never rest.

There are continual changes in demand and supply, calling for continual adjustment of prices.[a] This continual adjustment of prices is provided by the market. Whenever there is an excess of demand over supply the market raises the price, and in every excess of supply over demand it lowers the price. This equates supply and demand, makes the prices genuine and integrates production with consumption throughout the economy. The *price mechanism* includes both the "given" *price structures* required for economic efficiency as well as the *market* for adjusting the prices to keep them genuine.

However, all this assumes *perfect competition*. Perfect competition does not allow anyone to influence prices. This is what is meant by their being "given." Individual buyers and sellers are unable to change the prices. They have to accept them as they are. We will consider why in chapters 6 and 7.

---

[a]It might seem that there would have to be continuous changes in almost all prices. Fortunately this problem is reduced to manageable proportions because temporary changes in supply and demand are absorbed by changes in inventories.

## Chapter Five

# Market and Management

"Economists claim that the market is an instrument for serving the public good. Are they so naive that they refuse to see that the market is created by the capitalist regime for the exploitation of the weak by the strong?" That argument is found in the speeches and writing of many intellectuals, remarkably enough, by people of very different outlooks. In this chapter we will shed some light on this problem, dispel misunderstandings, and explain what economists have to say about it. Then we will investigate defects in the functioning of the market and ways of correcting them. From there, we will discuss efficient governmental economic policy.

We have seen how an ideal market generates processes that bring about integrated economic efficiency. Some mysterious force may seem to be involved here; but the price and market mechanism is only a technique for bringing to bear on each other the decisions of the producers and the consumers. Working through the prices these lead, as if by mathematical logic, to economic efficiency. The market is nothing more than an instrument for managing the economy, and as such we must examine its characteristics.

Management can be centralized or decentralized. Centralization in its most extreme form extends to the manager the full authority of decision and operation in every detail. Those under his authority must act in accordance with his instructions, with no authority of their own. At the other extreme, the decentralization spreads authority among all levels of management. Every submanager carries out his task as he sees fit.

Each method has its advantages and its drawbacks. An apparent advantage of centralization is that with all the information required for a decision collected in one central place, the general manager can weigh all the factors systematically and consistently, and so reach rational decisions. But there are drawbacks. The concentration of the information in one place is a difficult and complex process, in the course of which errors may be made. Even if the manager is perfectly rational and makes no logical errors, his decisions may be based on defective information, and will not be effective. Then, because the authority is entirely in the hands of the general manager, an intricate structure has to be built for transmitting orders as well as for checking on their performance. It is in the nature of things that such a complex, indeed dizzying, structure must develop distortions and imperfections.

These flaws in centralization are not too serious in a small organization, which of course requires limited information and supervision. But the larger the organization the greater the distortions. That is why, as organizations increase in size, there is a tendency for more and more decentralization to be incorporated.

But decentralization also has disadvantages. It requires that each submanager be supplied with the information required for rational decisionmaking within the limits of his authority. Accordingly, in decentralization, a complicated communications system must be set up. Furthermore, conflicts can arise between submanagers. In this case it is, of course, necessary to put the objectives of the organization above the interests and even the efficiency of any single branch. However, submanagers naturally tend to work for the benefit of their own branches. Thus it is necessary to construct the management system so as to minimize conflicts.

It is possible to consider human society as an economic organization consisting of innumerable consumers and producers. This is the largest possible organization. Theoretically, the management of this enormous organization could be centralized or decentralized.

A centralized economy is generally referred to as a planned economy.[a] A completely centralized national economy is still only an imaginary construct, in spite of the fabulous developments of science and technology. The use of electronic computers will not help much even if their speed and powers of storage of information should increase infinitely, for the fundamental problem is the gathering of the information. We have no way of collecting and concentrating such a vast amount of constantly changing information—especially that which deals with the nuances of consumer preferences—and arranging it in a manner that will allow rational decisionmaking. Only one large organization is basically centralized, the army. But even in the army there is decentralization. And it must be remembered that the problems of society are much greater and more complex than those of the army.

A pure market mechanism is at the opposite extreme—it is a *complete decentralization*. Every individual is free to determine his own behavior in pro-

---

[a]Planning is only one of the functions of management. The main functions are planning, execution, coordination, and control. It is clear that the widely used term "planned economy" refers to a managed economy. As we shall see below, the term refers to economies which make use of various degrees of centralization.

duction or in consumption. An individual consumer does not need anything remotely approaching the information that is essential for central planning. It is sufficient for him to know the market prices of inputs and outputs, and the technical possibilities for transforming inputs into outputs in his specialty. The price structure indicates the degree to which the factors of production and the products are needed by others. The individual is not concerned with who needs them, or where or for what purpose or in what quantities. This information, vital for central management, is superfluous for the market mechanism.

Thus, the decentralized market system overcomes problems that are unsolvable by centralization. While acting in his own interest, the individual will satisfy the conditions of economic efficiency. Prices indicate to the consumer the relative marginal utilities and the marginal rates of substitution. If he purchases too little of product A and too much of product B, he will be hurting himself most of all because he will not be maximizing utility. Thus there is an incentive that leads every consumer toward achieving economic efficiency in the economy as a whole.

The same holds for the producer. If a producer employs too few workers—or too many—so that the value of the marginal output exceeds, or falls short of, the wage, he will not be maximizing his profit. He himself gets hurt. Thus there is an incentive for every producer to work unconsciously for the efficiency of the economy as a whole.

To summarize, the decentralized price mechanism is better suited than is a centralized management for achieving integrated economic efficiency. Completely centralized management is just not feasible.

Those who have tried, and are now trying, to operate a centralized economy are forced to compromise and extend authority to lower levels. This has been the experience of the socialist East European countries. Even so, a partial centralization requires criteria to determine what decisions may be made at lower levels. But for economic efficiency, these decisions must be based on free-market prices. Only free-market prices can reflect the preferences of the consumer and the marginal rates of transformation between alternative products.

For ideological reasons, the socialist countries have severely limited the use of the market mechanism. Required levels of output are fixed, in physical terms, and a system of prizes and penalties set up for surpassing or failing to achieve these norms or goals. But physical instructions cannot faithfully reflect changing subjective preferences. Moreover, managerial control based on rewards and penalties, and specific goals, encourages a concentration only on performing the explicit instructions and ignoring, even consciously, the achievement of other, no-less-important objectives. When firms are assigned output quotas, in meeting them they find it easy and even tempting to sacrifice quality. If, in response, quality criteria are imposed in physical terms they can only be partial, selective and inadequate. For example, if a minimum thickness of a product is required, inferior material may be used to make it up. If, however, the nature of the raw material is specified, then the manager can "economize" on the size of the product, and so on.

The price mechanism solves the problem of effective performance. When perfect market prices prevail, and every firm tries to produce that which in quantity and quality will bring maximum profit, then management decisions will conform to consumer preferences, taking into consideration the costs of production. Top management needs to give submanagement one directive only—to strive toward maximum profit, given the existing set of prices. Any additional directive will bring about distortions and departures from economic efficiency. Thus, the most efficient possible planning system is precisely that which is based, as far as possible, on the price structure of a perfect market.

Barter transactions were a primitive market mechanism. However, barter was by its nature inefficient; each seller had to seek out each buyer. Only in the last few centuries did the means of exchange and technology make possible the growth and refinement of markets and of trade.

In this way the development of the refined price mechanism grew out of industrial development and in turn *made possible* the Industrial Revolution and the development of the capitalist system. Capitalism then came to be *identified* with the use of the price mechanism, even though there is no reason why it cannot be used in other economic systems, too.

It was because of this identification that, when dissatisfied with many aspects of capitalism, socialists set up socialist economies and felt that they had to abolish the market mechanism and replace it with centralized management. Economic efficiency and the level of public welfare fell rapidly. In the last few years there has been some dissipation of the ideological fog that has obscured understanding of the market. In the socialist countries it is being recognized more and more that to refrain from using the price mechanism because it is "capitalistic" is no more sensible than to boycott electricity because it too was developed by capitalists. In recent years the East European countries have been gradually adopting the price mechanism, integrating it into their planning. However, these beginnings have been modest, meeting internal opposition from both communist ideologists and bureaucratic pressure groups.

Nevertheless, in capitalist as well as in developing countries, there are influential circles opposed to the price and market system. These circles either have a very foggy understanding of the market, or represent those who benefit from activities that would not survive the use of the price system.

The opposition to using the price system is bolstered by the fact that in many countries perverted market prices prevent achievement of economic efficiency. The appropriate response would be to remove these distortions from the market. But opponents of the price system hasten to conclude that the market itself should be abolished.

The price system can function properly only if certain conditions are satisfied. When the proper conditions do not prevail the government must intervene and engage in some degree of central management. This is not rejecting or even avoiding the use of the market. It is, rather, a way of improving its effectiveness. Management can be of great use where the market mechanism cannot do the job. But only a proper understanding of how the market mechanism works can tell us where this is the case, and how management and the market can work together.

## Chapter Six

# Improving the Market Mechanism

Although each consumer and each producer exercises his own judgment and preferences, the market mechanism can bring about the integrated efficiency of the economy as a whole. However, two basic conditions must be satisfied if this is to work. The first condition is that the prices be *genuine*—so as to bring equality between demand and supply. The second condition is that they must also be *correct*—they must correctly represent the marginal cost of production. In a free market, prices are genuine; but for prices to be correct there must be perfect competition. A principal responsibility of government is to maintain both of these conditions.

### Ensuring Genuine Prices

"Why do you charge 40¢ for a pound of apples, when across the street they are only 20¢?" complains a customer.

"Why don't you buy them there?" answers the grocer.

"He's out of them."

"Well," answers the grocer, "if I were out of them, I'd be prepared to mark mine down to 10¢."

When a price is too low it has no meaning. Demand exceeds supply and the product cannot be freely bought at the marked price. There is pressure to raise the price until supply and demand are equal. On the other hand, when a price is too high, producers cannot sell freely and there is pressure to lower the price until demand equals supply.

Rigid prices will not balance demand and supply. Some would-be buyers and sellers will be unsatisfied. The marginal rates of substitution and transformation will be unbalanced. Only flexible prices can yield genuine prices. Freezes, price controls and other barriers to price flexibility are not in the public interest.[a] When genuine prices do not obtain, the government should remove the barriers to price adjustment.

We often find governments infringing this principle themselves. For example, during inflation due to excess demand, they may try to "freeze" prices! These prices are, of course, too low to be genuine, and demand becomes excessive. To prevent too inequitable and irresponsible a determination of who is able to buy and who is not, a rationing system automatically follows. Rationing is detrimental to industrial efficiency. Prices which are too low do not reflect the marginal preferences of consumers and rationing does not distribute goods and services according to the marginal rates of substitution.

In this situation those people for whom the marginal substitutability of a rationed product is low would sell a part of their ration to people for whom the marginal substitutability is high. Such transactions frustrate the purpose of the freeze since the effective "black market" prices would replace the official "frozen" prices. They would nevertheless improve efficiency in consumption.

But even if such trading were to balance completely the marginal substitutabilities between all products, it would still not bring integrated economic efficiency. The marginal substitutabilities would be in proportion to the black market and free market prices. The producers, however, would adjust output to make their marginal transformabilities equal to the ratios between the *official* or frozen prices. The marginal transformabilities of the rationed products would be below the marginal substitutabilities. There will not be the required equality between the marginal rates of transformation in production and the marginal rates of substitution in consumption. Consumers would be willing to pay a price higher than the marginal cost, and producers would gladly increase their output at that higher price. As long as there are price controls, trading will flourish outside the official market, even though it is illegal. Many governments that impose price controls have learned to permit trading in the parallel market to improve economic efficiency. But complete and integrated economic efficiency can be achieved only by completely abandoning the controls.

### Ensuring Correct Prices

In a perfect competition situation, no individual is large enough to influence any price significantly by limiting sales or purchases. The producer can manufacture and the consumer can buy any amount of any product whatsoever. The factors of production can be freely transferred from industry to industry and from firm to firm. Producers and consumers enjoy complete information on the profitability of production and purchase of any product.

These conditions will never be fully realized. It is still, however, possible to come close enough to them for the market mechanism to constitute

[a]"Freezing" does not deal with the causes of the inflation if the cause is excess demand.

the best available means for approaching economic efficiency. The role of the government is to promote perfect competition.

### Control over Business Restrictions

A monopoly is an economic unit that takes advantage of its size to raise prices by limiting sales. A monopsony is an economic unit that takes advantage of its size to lower market prices by limiting purchases.

When a monopoly sells an additional unit, this lowers the price of all the units it sells, reducing the marginal revenue below the price.[b] To maximize profit a monopoly produces that output which equates marginal cost to marginal revenue. But, as we have seen, this marginal revenue is less than the market price. Though the consumers' marginal substitutabilities are based on the market prices, the monopoly's marginal transformability is based on the marginal revenues. This inequality impairs market efficiency. The resulting (marginal) loss can be measured by the difference between the price and the marginal cost of production. The price shows the degree to which the consumers are eager for a product, and the marginal cost reflects the value of alternative products foregone. A price higher than the marginal cost means that the output is too small.

When a monopsony buys an additional unit of a factor, its price rises. The marginal cost of buying an additional unit is therefore higher than the price. To maximize profits, the monopsony, like any other firm, adjusts its purchases so as to equate the marginal cost to the marginal revenue. Because the marginal cost is higher than the price, a monopsony will buy less than is required for economic efficiency. The marginal revenue, which is equal to the price of the product (unless the monopsony is also a monopoly) does measure the degree to which consumers are eager for the product, but the price of the factor bought by the monopsony, which is what the producer of the factor gets for it, reflects the value of alternative products foregone. The monopsonistic restriction, just like the monopolistic restriction, thus makes the price of the final product higher than the value of alternative products foregone, and this means that the output is too low. Of course, if a firm is both a monopoly and a monopsony, the output will be too low on both counts.

A monopoly that consists of several firms can be disbanded. If possible, such combinations should be prevented in the first place. Indeed, some countries have laws against monopolies; but in any event making it easier for firms to enter an industry hinders monopolies and monopsonies.

Laws can also work against oligopolies and oligopsonies, i.e., indus-

---

[b]Assume that when 10 units are produced, the price is $20 per unit, and for 11 units the price is $19. There is an increase in revenue from $200 to $209, with a marginal revenue of $9. The additional unit is indeed sold for $19, but the other 10 units are now sold for $19 instead of $20 each, resulting in a loss of $10. The marginal revenue of the monopoly is, thus, the price ($19) minus the loss from the reduction in price of the other units ($10). This comes to $9.

tries with only a few large firms who have to take into account not only their own influence on prices but also the effects of each one's decisions on the reactions of the others in the industry. Under these conditions, efficiency can be even more seriously damaged because in addition to restrictions on output, price rigidity prevails. This is caused by the fear that lowering a price would result in a sharp price war.

Public utilities are "natural monopolies." In a natural monopoly the average cost of production decreases as its output expands. Several small electric companies in a region would have greater total production costs than would one large company, so that it is more efficient to have one large one. In any case the larger firm will be able to undercut any smaller firms. The firms naturally become large enough to be able to influence the price of electricity significantly. It is *naturally* monopolistic. It does not have to combine with other firms in a conspiracy to establish a monopoly.

To prevent a utility from setting rates that are too high for economic efficiency, public commissions regulate their rates, ideally setting them at a level at which prices equal marginal cost, maximizing economic efficiency. But in a natural monopoly average costs decrease with increasing output. The marginal cost will, therefore, be less than the average cost.[c] Hence, if the rule is followed of setting price equal to marginal cost, the utility's income would be less than its expenditures. This leads to a very important conclusion: For economic efficiency, a natural monopoly must operate at a loss. This loss must be made up by the government.

In practice, public utilities are permitted to set their prices at a level that will allow them a profit comparable to those of firms under free competition. This is preferable to no regulation, but it does not yield economic efficiency. The price reflects the average cost, not the marginal cost, which is lower.

Regulating a public utility or other natural monopoly in this way is equivalent to having a price equal to the marginal cost, and on top of that a tax per unit equal to the difference between the marginal cost and the average cost (including a normal profit) to cover the loss. It makes no difference whether the government imposes the tax and gives the proceeds to the public utility, or allows the utility to collect the tax itself as part of the price charged for the product.

Whoever collects the tax still is responsible for impairing economic efficiency by raising the price above the marginal cost. It would be more rational for the government to cover the loss even if it has to impose additional taxation to raise the money. It should then impose the additional taxes where they do the least harm to overall economic efficiency. This would mean an increase in some

---

[c]Assume that 10 units are manufactured at the average cost of $4, with a total cost of $40. When 11 units are manufactured, the average cost falls to $3.90, with total cost now $42.90. The marginal cost is therefore $2.90, which is less than the average cost.

*other* taxes, unless the tax on this product, equal to the difference between the marginal and average cost, should happen to be the one tax, of all those available to the government, which does the least damage to overall economic efficiency.[d]

It is commonly believed that if a public company shows a profit it is operating well. But this criterion of efficiency is valid only if the company is operating under perfect competition, side-by-side with private firms. For a natural monopoly, the making of a profit signals *inefficient* operation from the point of view of the economy as a whole. It shows that the price is above the average cost and, therefore, even more above the marginal cost.

Government regulation of the prices utilities charge may look like an intervention that interferes with the market. This is an illusion. It is in fact the monopolistic combinations and the monopolistic behavior of firms that damage economic efficiency. Government interventions here only modify interferences with the market mechanism and so serve to reduce the monopolistic restrictions.

One by-product of monopoly is price discrimination. In Israel the railray system, for example, sets very low freight charges for phosphates; favored firms receive loans at specially low rates of interest; farmers get water more cheaply than industry; and so on. Price discrimination is of course possible only with products that cannot be transferred from consumer to consumer. A buyer will not willingly pay a high price for a product when he can get it for less by re-purchasing it from a favored customer.

If all prices equaled marginal cost, discrimination would not be possible. Discrimination demonstrates that economic efficiency has been breached; the price mechanism is operating imperfectly and there is a need for intervention to correct the flaws.

### Improved Information

Complete information on prices and possibilities of production is required to ensure that the marginal rates of substitution and of transformation are the same for every producer and consumer. A consumer may not know that at a nearby shop he can get what he wants at a lower price; a producer may not know that what he plans to produce is already being made by others so that the price will fall below that level on which he calculated his profits. Where information is insufficient, the inequality between the marginal rates of substitution and of transformation will be upset.

Government intervention to ensure the proper working of the price mechanism needs to focus also on spreading appropriate information, publicizing statistics, data, projections and estimates, and it should tax and fine the spreading of misleading information.

[d]The question of efficient taxation will be discussed in Chapter 9.

# Chapter Seven

# Limitations of the Perfect Market

The price mechanism can bring the economy to *integrated* economic efficiency but not to *overall* economic efficiency. For this the government must help.

### Adjusting Prices to Externalities

Up to now it has been assumed that production costs are borne only by the producer of a product, and that the pleasures derived from consumption are enjoyed only by the purchaser. This is not always so. Some products have *external effects.*

An electric power plant produces smoke which disturbs residents. Part of the burden of producing electricity, then, is borne by those who live near the plant. Similarly, a telephone benefits not only the subscriber, but others who can call him up. These *external costs* and *external benefits* are to be distinguished from the *internal* or *private* costs and benefits. The external cost of producing electricity is the damage caused to suffering neighbors. The external benefit from installing telephones is the increase in enjoyment of others.

The *social* benefit or cost is a combination of the internal and the external. Overall economic efficiency requires equality for each product between the *marginal social cost* and the *marginal social benefit;* and consequently, for each pair of products, equality between the *marginal social rate of transformation* and the *marginal social rate of substitution.* If only the marginal private cost and the marginal private benefit are considered, the economy will not reach overall economic efficiency.

For overall efficiency the consumer must pay not only the private cost to the producer (which corresponds to the harm caused by the using up of the factors of production) but also for the external costs—the damage to others. He must similarly be credited for the external benefits. One way of doing this is to tax operations with external costs and subsidize those with external benefits by amounts equal to the marginal external costs or benefits, as the case may be.

If the electric company must compensate residents for smoke damage, it will pass on the charge to the consumer. And if the payment equals the damage, the company will try to mitigate the damage—by decreasing the smoke or by moving the plant so as to reduce the payment. It will do this as long as the cost of avoiding the damage is less than the damage avoided—since that will be the compensation payment avoided. Such adjustment would bring the marginal social cost of avoiding the smoke damage into equality with the marginal social benefit from smoke abatement. An appropriate system of charges for external damage will lead to the most efficient degree of diminution of damage from pollution. What remains will be the *optimum degree of pollution*—that pollution which it is not worthwhile removing because the costs would exceed the benefits. Similarly, to obtain the maximum social benefit from telephone services the charges must be set *below* the marginal private cost by an amount equal to the marginal external benefit.

### Maintaining Price Stability and Full Employment

Stability of the price level requires that demand should not exceed production (Gross National Product) at full employment, otherwise prices rise. Price stability can of course exist during unemployment, but full economic efficiency can be achieved *only if price stability is combined with full employment.* Unemployment can also coexist with inflation.

During an inflation, money loses purchasing power. Consumers hurry to buy goods, racing against the rising prices; and producers hurry to buy up raw materials. Producers also tend to hoard the products, waiting to sell at higher prices.

If the expectations are identical for all producers and consumers, they would continue to respond to a single expected price structure or set of prices, and economic efficiency would be maintained. But in practice, because of the natural uncertainties of the future, the expectations are not identical. Different people have different price expectations and therefore respond to different price structures. Inflation therefore must diminish economic efficiency.

Unemployment is, by definition, an extreme case of economic inefficiency. No sacrifice of alternative products is required to increase the output of any product by using unemployed factors. The correct price for every product that could be produced by unemployed factors of production is *zero,* and the correct price for the unemployed factors of production themselves is also zero. Society would gain from the employment of unused factors of production as long as their marginal product is of any value at all. But the producer has to pay the market price for the unemployed factors, so it is not worth his while to employ them. It is therefore one of the principal tasks of governmental economic policy to combine full employment with a stable price level.[a]

[a]This topic will be treated in more detail in Chapter 18.

### Attaining Social Objectives

Government is not concerned just with economic efficiency, it also has sociopolitical obligations. The way income has been divided among the population has distressed mankind throughout history.

In a market economy one's income consists of payments for the services of the factors of production that he owns. It will therefore depend in the first place on the market price of a unit of each kind of productive service and in the second place on how many of these units are provided by the factors of production that he owns. The more important of these factors of production is each person's own labor power, the services which he provides, and for which he is paid in wages or salaries.

The resulting division of income may not be socially acceptable. Accordingly, it is up to the government to make it more acceptable by some redistribution of income. In doing this, care must be taken to see that the least harm possible is done to economic efficiency.[b]

### Consumption and Investment

The consumer usually prefers not to consume all his income but to save a part of it. He will receive interest on his savings, as compensation for postponing consumption. He can maximize his benefit by increasing his saving as long as the marginal utility lost in postponing consumption is less than the marginal utility gained from the increased future income, including the interest, up to the point where the two marginal utilities have become equal. Those who put money into investment projects will do so up to the point where the investment will yield no more from the marginal investment than the interest he has to pay on the money invested (or has to forego in not lending it out instead of investing it). The rate of interest governs how much every individual will save or invest. A properly working price system will determine the rate of interest in exactly the same way as other prices, and this will bring about a determinate volume of saving and investment.

However, decisions about saving and about investment have far-reaching influences on the rate of economic growth, on price stability and unemployment, on the balance of payments, and on the levels of the living of future generations. There are, that is to say, external costs and benefits. Because of this many governments consider themselves entitled, and even duty bound, to intervene in the decisions that affect the division of the total social output between consumption and investment, and to influence consumption and investment in accordance with social objectives.

### Socially Preferred Products

We have been assuming that for economic efficiency in consumption, we must allow the consumer free choice between alternative products and

[b]A more detailed examination of these problems appears in chapters 8 and 20.

services. In this way, the consumer achieves his maximum utility. However, modern society places restrictions on this principle. A person addicted to drink who ignores his family obligations operates according to his personal preferences, but from a social point of view it is desirable to change his behavior. Similarly, the government forbids a person to deprive his children of basic education. The government also provides health services, and does not leave this concern entirely to the individual.

There are many ways in which the government can influence consumption. It can establish legislative and administrative controls (compulsory education and laws against the use of certain drugs). It can also make use of the price mechanism, providing subsidies (education, health, the postal service) and leveling taxes (alcoholic beverages). But in every case care must be taken if economic inefficiency is to be avoided.[c]

Taxes and subsidies are among the most important instruments of governmental intervention. Progressive taxes, falling more heavily on the rich, and subsidies to reduce the prices of products consumed by the poor, reduce inequality of income. Similarly, subsidies and tax reductions to investors, and income-tax allowances on interest paid to savers, will contribute to the encouragement of investing and saving. Taxes and subsidies can also help to stabilize the economy. In an inflation resulting from excess demand, taxes can serve as a brake and reduce the excess of demand. In the case of unemployment, a reduction in taxes or an increase in subsidies will stimulate demand, increase economic activity, and reduce the unemployment.

Taxes and subsidies can be applied both to income and to the sale of goods and services. In either case, they create gaps between the price paid by the buyer and the price received by the seller. But economic efficiency requires prices to be equal to marginal cost for everybody. (An exception is where the tax or subsidy is applied to goods and services with external costs or benefits so as to correct the prices for these external effects). Taxes and subsidies are therefore bound to damage economic efficiency. This damage is the price that has to be paid if the social priorities are to be achieved. In Chapters 9 and 17 we will discuss the principles governing tax and subsidy policy which minimize the damage to economic efficiency.

### Centralization and Decentralization

Decentralization by means of the price mechanism is indeed the most efficient method of dealing with the great complexity of the economy. However, there are certain situations where the centralized method is preferable. There are goods and services where the individual consumer's benefit does not depend on

[c]A notorious example of an inefficient system is the prohibition in America in the twenties of the production and distribution of intoxicating liquors. Prohibition led to the development of an underground black market, an increase in crime, and the enrichment of a few—and it was finally repealed.

how much he spends on them. Such are defense, police, justice and so on. The individual consumer therefore has no incentive to pay. Consequently the market mechanism is not able to bring about the appropriate outputs. Only a public authority, like the government, can do this.

The price mechanism works most efficiently in dealing with such production and consumption as is subject to minor adjustments to ever-changing conditions. If output can be increased or decreased by just a few units; if a plant can be added or closed down in an industry where there are already many plants—these are small changes. An increase or decrease in the consumption of a specific product, either by an individual consumer or by several consumers, may then constitute a small change. Economic efficiency is obtained through the price mechanism by relatively small and continuous adjustments in inputs and outputs, each adjustment being made on the basis of *a set of prices*—a price structure.

But there also exist large undertakings which, by their nature, cannot be divided into small changes. A new deep-water port or a new industrial center are large projects that must be treated as a whole. They are *indivisible*. They are not merely the sum of a series of small changes. Such large enterprises cannot be carried out on the basis of *a given price structure.* This is because it changes the market conditions and brings about significant changes in the prices. The centralized method may then be more efficient. Planners, unlike the market mechanism, can take into account *changes* in relative prices, and in other economic conditions, resulting from the project itself.

This issue must not be confused with monopoly. A monopoly is also a large body that influences the level of prices in its sphere of interest; however a monopoly need not involve indivisibility. If its activity can be divided, the monopoly can be broken down into smaller companies. This is not the case with big projects, such as the ones cited above, which cannot be split into a series of small changes.

### Obstacles to the Flow of Information

An essential condition for economic efficiency in a decentralized system is that every unit receive the information necessary for proper decisions. The information must therefore be freely available and flow without hindrance wherever it may be required. For the centralized method, however, the information need only reach the one focal point: the general manager or administrator.

Sometimes the information is not easily made available. The costs of distribution may be too great, exceeding the gain in efficiency. It is then more efficient for the information to be sent to one central location, and the decisions left to one manager. Under these conditions, the centralized system is the more efficient.

For example, in planning a road network, the planner needs to know the geology of the area, the expected number of trips from point to point, the resources available for investment in the network and so on. The planner can then give instructions to different people engaged in constructing different parts of the network, without giving each one all the information he has. These subcontractors carry out the planner's instructions. If all the subcontractors had all the information available to the planner, each one would be in a position to plan the whole network—in the identical way as all the other subcontractors (since there is only one best way, which they would all figure out)—including the part that each knows he would do best. Each would then know what he should do. But we cannot suppose that they all could obtain all the information and understand it the same way. Only centralized management is appropriate in such a case.

In other cases it is not necessary, and usually not even possible, for all the information to be concentrated at one point, and even if it were it would be far too much for the center to be able to handle. This is where a decentralized system is more efficient.

In the last few chapters we have considered some conditions that are liable to interfere with the ability of the price mechanism to achieve economic efficiency. The charge is often made that the real trouble lies in the economy being based on the price mechanism in the first place! As we have shown, it is essential to distinguish between the price mechanism, in its technical sense, and the conditions necessary for its efficient operation. If these conditions do not exist it cannot work efficiently. But if the whole price mechanism were abolished efficiency would be harmed even more. The sensible thing is not to reject the price mechanism as a whole but to repair its defects and to improve it.

We have also seen that even if we have complete economic efficiency, the results may not be what the society would like. When this is the case, government intervention through the price mechanism may help. Such intervention will indeed reduce economic efficiency, but the loss in economic efficiency may be more than offset by the value of the social objectives gained. In any case, intervention should take forms that minimize the damage to economic efficiency. And where centralization is more efficient than decentralization, it is the centralized system that should be used.

In the next chapter we will examine more carefully the nature of the services that can be rendered to society by the market mechanism and those that can be rendered by administrative methods, and how these are related to each other.

# Chapter Eight

# Economic Planning

The concept of economic planning, in its purest form, grows out of the notion that the good society can be built only after *prices, markets, money,* and *profits* have been abolished. Instead of production being based on the pursuit of profits and the exploitation of others, society's resources would be directed rationally toward making things people need. "Production for use" is put forward as an alternative to "production for profit." Everything would be distributed by a central authority in an economy of pure administration, with subordinate managers receiving specific and detailed instructions from the center.

As we saw in Chapter 5, modern economies are so complex that no single central administrative body can manage them efficiently. No one body is able to gather all the necessary information on the resources at the economy's disposal, on the ability and willingness of workers to perform different kinds of work, on the infinite nuances of consumers' preferences, on the technological possibilities of production of all products and their transportation and distribution among the public, and finally, on the continual changes that each of these factors constantly undergoes. All this information is an essential prerequisite for a centralized administrative body that is supposed to give detailed instructions to each of the factors of production as to what should be produced, in what quantities, by what production process, and so on.

There is no better demonstration of the unworkability of this system than the failure of all attempts to set up and operate a centrally administered economy. The outstanding example is the terrible experience suffered by the citizens of the Soviet Union in the years immediately following the Russian Revolution, from which they were rescued only when the system of money, prices and profits was reinstated as part of the New Economic Policy (Lenin's NEP) in 1921.

The lessons learned from this devastating experience brought about an almost universal (but tacit) rejection of "planning" in its original intent of "the introduction of rationality into the anarchy of the market" by means of a completely centralized administration. Indeed, in the theoretical field, there are signs in recent years in the socialist countries of Eastern Europe of a tendency even to exaggerate the advantages of the market, price and profit mechanism. In practice these instruments are used there only in small part and with great hesitation.

In Chapter 5 we distinguished between the administrative system and the market mechanism. An economy in which there is no market mechanism whatsoever would be a purely administrative economy. At the other pole, an economy in which there is no administration whatsoever and which uses only the market mechanism to guide production and distribution would be a pure market economy. In such an economy one can find no authority telling anyone what to produce or how to produce it. All production would be carried out by individuals who buy uncompleted products on a free market, do some work on these, and then sell them to others, making their living from the difference in the prices. There would be no employers and no employees, no instructions and no organizations of the kind found in every firm in any actual economy.

There has never been a pure market economy of this sort, nor can there ever be one. But the production process is executed far more efficiently in firms operated with some degree of managerial authority. Management increases the efficiency of production to such an extent that it more than compensates for the limitations it places on individual freedom. But wherever the market mechanism affords greater efficiency as well as greater personal freedom, the market mechanism is certainly preferable.

In light of this, and in light of the failure of experiments with the pure administrative method, the word "planning" has a changed meaning. It has come to stand for the determination by some high authority of the degree and the manner in which the economy will make use of the market mechanism and the degree to which it will make use of the administrative system. These two mechanisms, *market* and *administration,* are instruments that can be used side by side. The real problem of planning is to organize that combination of the two techniques which will bring about the highest level of overall economic efficiency. Planning, in its new meaning, now stands for the determination of both the social objectives and the most effective combination of instruments for achieving them.

The proper combination of administration and the market mechanism can be conceived of as a goal that can be reached by two different paths, starting from opposite directions. One path consists of the gradual introduction of increasing degrees of administration into a pure market economy. The other path consists of the gradual introduction of market mechanisms into a purely administrative economy. We will first review the steps by which market mechanisms can be introduced into a purely administrative economy.

The first step in breaking away from a purely administrative system is for the central administrative body to give the lower-level managers *goals* or *targets* instead of detailed instructions. This is a decisive step toward the decentralization of authority. It constitutes, in effect, a renunciation of the basic idea of pure administration—the idea that a central administrative body can piece together the giant jigsaw puzzle of the economy. It is clear that the efficiency of the system is damaged when some managers fail to achieve their goals or if the actual target is surpassed. In this second case, other targets must have failed of accomplishment if the plan had been based on full utilization of the available resources. Over-achievement by some must result in under-achievement by others whose resources have been preempted by the over-achievers.

The second step, whose importance in improving efficiency is almost as great as the first step, is the replacement of specific targets in physical terms by targets expressed in money values. This step is being undertaken, albeit with great indecisiveness, in the Soviet Union and in other East European socialist countries. With this method, firms cannot claim unsold and unsaleable output as contributing toward meeting their set targets.

The third step is to free from central administrative authority altogether any competitive sectors of the economy in which there are only small firms employing few workers and producing goods and services that do not particularly interest the authorities. The inputs and outputs of these sectors can be included in the total plan, but only as *estimates,* because the individual firms have no set allocations.

The fourth step is the release from the authority of central administration of all sectors and branches of the economy in which, although the firms are large, there are significant numbers of them, so that they have to compete with each other, and they produce goods and services which have no externalities and are of no special interest to the government. Instead of giving these sectors specific detailed instructions, it would suffice to provide them only with *indicative* targets and directives. These conditions can be discussed and negotiated by the government and the representatives of the firms in each industry. The government has many ways of applying persuasion and pressure to get the firms to cooperate, but the government's directives do not have to be accepted in their entirety. This method is known as *indicative planning.* It is not found in the socialist countries of Eastern Europe but is primarily in use in France. There are, of course, divergent opinions over the contribution of this method to France's economic development after World War II.

The fifth step is release of the remaining firms from centralized control. This control was perhaps justified on account of their size, inasmuch as large firms, aspiring to maximum profits, tend to behave like monopolies, limiting their output to a volume less than that required for economic efficiency. Another reason for exercizing control over these industries may be some external effects of their operations. However, at this stage it is also possible to operate with a decentralized method, benefiting from its advantages without sacrificing any of the purposes for which the controls were imposed. These can be achieved by appropriate adjustments in the price structure: levying taxes, providing subsidies in accordance with external costs and benefits, and formulating price policies that will induce monopolies to produce at a level where their marginal cost equals the price.

The sixth step is the abolition of centralized controls imposed on *consumers* to achieve objectives desired by the authorities. As in the previous step, such controls can be removed without abandoning the aims of government policy if appropriate changes are made in the price structure—namely by granting subsidies to those products whose consumption the government wants to encourage, and levying taxes on those products whose consumption the government wants to discourage. This may be called *market intervention.*

A distinction must be made between intervention by the authorities for the benefit of the general public, and intervention on behalf of pressure groups that have political influence. Such a distinction cannot, however, be easily made, as the pressure groups generally maintain that the privileges they claim are in the general public interest.

The seventh step is the cancelling of indicative planning insofar as it tries to achieve its objectives by persuasion. The only part of indicative planning that will then remain is that which deals with the collection of estimates and forecasts of the inputs and outputs of firms and industries and the examination of the consistency of the forecasts with one another. The accessibility to the public of the collected information will enable firms to check the reliability of their own forecasts and to adjust their programs accordingly. But now all that is left is *information services.* Those still interested in appearing to preserve some kind of "planning" will prefer to call this "informational planning."

Once we have developed methods for correcting monopolistic behavior and of superimposing social over individual preferences, and have established information services, nothing remains of indicative planning but the attempt by the central authority to improve the programs of the various companies, even though it knows less than the directors of the companies about the local conditions. At this stage, the indicative plan is nothing more than an anachronistic carryover from the purely administrative system.

The seven steps we have surveyed all serve to increase economic efficiency and improve public welfare. The central administrative method is transformed into the method of the price and market mechanism, without sacrificing any one of the social objectives. The question now is: What remains of administration?

To answer this question we must start from the opposite pole, from the pure market economy, and see how the introduction of administrative methods could improve the efficiency of the economy. We will consider a step-by-step introduction of administration and note how it can improve efficiency and further social objectives. We should not be surprised if, in the end, we find ourselves in the same position that we reached by starting from the opposite pole of pure administration. These steps can now be sketched more briefly than when we examined the first path.

Before we begin we must point out that the price mechanism cannot operate at all without the administrative method first ensuring several basic conditions, namely security of property (social and private), enforcement of contracts and all that goes with these institutions.

The first step for improving the economic efficiency of the pure market is to permit small units to be set up, within which only the administrative method operates—namely, small firms. This means permitting one man to employ other men for a wage. This would have been prohibited in a "pure market economy"—perhaps as "exploitation" or "wage slavery." At this stage big firms are not permitted to do this, in order to prevent monopolies from being set up.

Step two is the prevention of monopolies from developing by prohibiting trade restrictions or monopolistic combinations of firms, by increasing mobility, by spreading information, and the like. After these measures have been taken, the setting up of (administratively managed) larger firms can be permitted without fear that monopolies will develop.

The third step is the introduction of central administrative machinery to ensure full employment and price stability. These are the tools of fiscal and monetary policy.

The fourth step is to permit the establishment of natural monopolies as administered bodies. However, in order to prevent efficiency from being damaged by monopolistic practices controls must be applied, with appropriate regulation of their pricing policies.

Step five is the application of *market intervention* for superimposing the (social) preferences of the authorities on the private preferences of the consumers. This is to be accomplished by an appropriate system of taxes and subsidies.

The sixth step is the establishment of a central administrative mechanism for direct management of economic enterprises, i.e., administration in the purest sense. This would be applied not to all consumers and all producers, but only in those areas of activity where the administrative method is more efficient.

The seventh and final step is the systematic centralization of estimates, projections and forecasts to check on the consistency between the programs of the different firms, in an information service. This is connected with action to prevent misleading information from being spread through advertising and public relations activities in the information media.

All of these steps increase social welfare and improve economic efficiency, compared with the pure market system starting point. In the course of this process we also achieved some additional social objectives. The same final state of affairs was also reached by the seven steps from the purely centralized administration. At this point we have achieved the most efficient combination of market and management. Any further step beyond this point, in either direction, would only damage welfare. If we continue in the direction of more administration, and introduce, for example, "indicative planning," or if we continue in the pure market direction by giving up "informational planning," or by abandoning the instruments for stabilizing the price level and ensuring full employment, welfare would certainly be diminished.

The foregoing imaginary trips from imaginary regimes of pure administration and pure market toward an ideal combination of the two principles of social organization bring out very clearly the nature of the methods and their specific advantages. But it is, after all, an abstract mental exercise. In the following chapter we shall spell out more explicitly the different practical ways in which the government, which is in itself an administrative and not a market mechanism, can go about making the best use of the market mechanism for better servicing both the preferences of the public and its own social objectives.

**Chapter Nine**

# Principles of Efficient Economic Policy

Economic policy has five main channels of action: (1) action *on behalf* of the market, directed at creating the basic conditions for the proper working of the price mechanism; (2) action *on* the market, directed at improving its functioning; (3) action *through* the market, directed at dealing with external effects and with social priorities by means of adjustments in the price structure; (4) action *within* the market, directed at achieving particular objectives as one of the participants in the market; and (5) action *outside* the market, directed at setting up centralized, administrative, economic mechanisms where these are more efficient than the decentralized market mechanisms.

### Action on Behalf of the Market

Only the government can create the conditions for the proper functioning of the market. For this it must provide effective legislation on which commercial transactions can be based, providing security of property rights and reducing uncertainty in business operations. The government must regulate the activities of organizations and institutions, private or public, which are powerful enough to be able to abuse the market and impair its proper functioning. The government must devise and improve laws in many varied fields directed at perfecting, stabilizing and simplifying the operation of the market mechanism and increasing its reliability.

The government must also support the distribution of truthful information on the possibilities of production and consumption and the quality of products and of their components while preventing false and misleading publicity.

### Action on the Market

As we have seen, there are a number of phenomena that are liable to disturb the proper functioning of the price mechanism. Price rigidity prevents the consumer from obtaining all he wants to buy at the given prices, and prevents the producer from selling all the output it is worth his while to produce. Monopoly and monopsony, price discrimination, administrative restrictions on the volume of trade, are all similarly harmful. The harm common to all these is that they prevent the market from establishing the socially desirable equality between the marginal rates of substitution in consumption (for consumers) and the marginal rate of transformation in production (for producers).

It is the government's responsibility to remove or neutralize forces that would distort the "correct" price structure required for economic efficiency. The government can eliminate monopolies, monopsonies, and cartels, both of buyers and of sellers, by prohibiting the setting of maximum or minimum prices and by outlawing price discrimination. The government can also ensure correct prices by operating directly on the market, buying and selling any quantities supplied or demanded at appropriate, marginal, social-cost prices. These would have to be provisional prices, adjusted from time to time to changes in cost and demand conditions.

There are those who believe that in order to ensure economic efficiency the government must intervene and fix both the quantities and the prices. For this they propose the setting up of teams of economists who will compute exact costs of production and prescribe both the outputs and the prices.[a] This is no way to achieve economic efficiency. No matter how exact the computations by the teams, it is quite impossible for them to take into account the continual changes in the conditions of production, to consider technological changes and determine their rate of adoption, or to anticipate the changes in demand.

"Fixed prices" and "correct prices" are mutually contradictory terms. Obtaining correct prices is possible only if the prices are not fixed but flexible. Fixing prices and outputs conflicts with the principle of prices changing in accordance with movements in cost and demand as these adjust to each other. Even if we could arrange for current computations to keep up with all changes in adjusting prices and outputs, the best they could do would be to achieve what is reached anyway by the price mechanism.

### Action through the Market: Taxes and Subsidies
The government acts through the market mechanism by applying taxes and subsidies, changing the prices so as to alter the behavior of producers and consumers. One must distinguish here between two cases: the case where the government wants to change the production and consumption of a *specific* product, and the case where the government wants to change the level of consumption *in general.*

---

[a]In Israel, a system similar to this operates in agriculture. Teams within the Ministry of Agriculture compute the costs of production, fix producers' prices, determine the areas to be cultivated and allocate the areas among the producers. Marketing councils operating under the authority of the Ministry of Agriculture regulate the flow of products going to the market (see Chapter 22).

**Changing Specific Consumption.** The government will want to change the output and consumption of a specific product if the product involves external benefits or costs, or because of a social preference. In these cases, a gap must be created between the price to the producer and the price to the consumer. If the quantity of output and consumption is to be increased, the price paid by the consumer must be reduced below the price received by the producer, and the government must provide a subsidy which will cover the difference between the two prices. For products having external benefits, the subsidy per unit of product should be equal to the marginal external benefits. Consumption will then be increased until there is equality between the marginal cost of production and the marginal *social* utility (the purchaser's marginal utility, plus the external marginal utility). On the other hand, when the purpose is to reduce output and consumption because of external costs, the same principle requires the price to the consumer to be higher than the marginal cost of production by the amount of the marginal external cost or disbenefit. The price will then be raised to equality with the marginal *social* cost.

**Changing Consumption in General.** Taxes and subsidies can be directed toward achieving general objectives not especially related to any specific product. In an inflation caused by excess demand, an increase in taxes can help to reduce the excess demand. In depression, subsidies can reduce unemployment. Such taxes and subsidies contribute to economic stability and thereby increase economic efficiency. They can also aid in achieving social objectives. For example, progressive taxation and subsidies to those with low incomes reduce the inequality of income.

Taxes and subsidies can thus help to achieve general or social objectives; however, as they are levied on incomes and on specific goods and services, they damage economic efficiency. This damage stems from the gap created between the price to the producer and the price to the consumer, which upsets the equality between the marginal substitutibility and the marginal transformability. To achieve the objectives of taxes and subsidies while minimizing the damage to economic efficiency, taxes and subsidies that have the least possible effect on the behavior of producers and consumers should be chosen. A tax that does not influence consumers' and producers' behavior is called a *neutral* tax.

A lump-sum tax is an outstanding example of a neutral tax. This is a tax levied on an individual at a fixed amount (not necessarily the same for everybody) without considering his income, his expenditures or his market behavior. Accordingly, such a tax will not affect the equality of the marginal rates of substitution to the marginal rates of transformation. A *per capita* tax (the same for everyone) increases the inequality of income, while a universal *per capita* subsidy reduces the inequality of income, again without diverting the economy from economic efficiency.

Taxes and subsidies levied against some goods and services but not against all are not neutral; they result in changes in price which cause consumers to shift from the taxed to the untaxed or more lightly taxed items. These are presumably less needed (and therefore not previously chosen) so that there is a decrease in economic efficiency. However, if the price change does not greatly influence the amount demanded or supplied, the departure from efficiency will be small.

A tax of this type, whose influence is small, is that on the rent of all land. Landowners cannot raise their rents because that would remove part of their land from being used at all. Accordingly, landowners will be forced to absorb the whole burden of the tax. The rent will remain at the original level, the use of the land will not change, and economic efficiency will remain undamaged. Increasing or decreasing taxes of this type alters the division of incomes and can contribute to the stabilization of the economy without touching economic efficiency. Taxes levied on goods consumed by rich people hurt efficiency very little, where the demand for these products does not depend much on the price. A tax of this type, since it falls on those with high incomes, is similar to a progressive income tax.

The greater the number of goods and services taxed, the less will be the consumer's opportunity of substituting untaxed goods for the taxed ones. There will be a smaller shift to inferior, untaxed substitutes, and a smaller loss of efficiency. The substitutes must be inferior or they would have been chosen even without the tax. If the tax is levied at an equal rate on all products, as well as on leisure, efficiency will not be affected at all, because consumers cannot avoid the tax by shifting from taxed products to any substitute. A general tax is thus a neutral tax. Income tax is a relatively efficient tax since it is equivalent to a tax on all the goods and services purchased out of the taxed income.

Income tax is not quite a general tax because it is not levied on the leisure of the worker. Leisure is thus made relatively cheaper. An income tax induces the worker to increase his leisure time, that is to say, to work less than is appropriate for economic efficiency.[b] Furthermore, the income tax is not levied on goods and services which the individual produces for himself. This too harms economic efficiency. The income tax also harms efficiency because it discriminates against saving, since the tax is usually levied not only on the income that is saved but also on its fruits—the future interest income.

A tax aimed at changing the consumption of a particular product may simultaneously serve to bring about a desired general change in overall con-

---

[b]This inclination to work less may be offset, or even more than offset, by an opposing tendency: with a reduction in after-tax income, people are inclined to work harder to make up for the loss. But even then less work is done than economic efficiency would call for, taking into account the lower net income. The marginal utility of leisure is less than the marginal utility of the alternative marginal product from working, though *both* marginal utilities may be higher for the worker who, because of the income tax, enjoys less goods as well as less leisure.

sumption. If the government is interested in raising the level of education and is also interested in increasing the income level of the poor—and the majority of people with low education levels are in low-income brackets—then educational subsidies granted to the children of the poor will serve both objectives together. This is a case where the subsidy serves two objectives at the same time—one specific (education), and the second general (division of income).

It is nevertheless necessary to distinguish between these two purposes or we can easily find ourselves with an inefficient tax. Assume, for example, that to increase the income of the poor, they are supplied with clothing at especially low prices. If for some reason we are particularly interested in increasing the consumption of clothing by the poor, then the policy achieves two purposes at the same time. But if there is no such special interest in clothing consumption, the measure is inefficient. The poor will no doubt benefit by getting more clothes, but the consumption of clothing will rise above the efficiency level. Their marginal substitutability of clothing for other goods and services will be reduced below that for other consumers, and below the marginal transformability of clothing into other goods and services. The greater the subsidy to clothing, the greater the harm to economic efficiency. It would be more efficient to give the same subsidy in the form of cash. They would then not be tempted to buy more clothing in order to get more subsidy, but would divide the money subsidy among different goods and services in the way they consider best. They would be better off, the gain coming entirely out of the greater efficiency of the economy.

The same logic applies to a bread subsidy given to bakers. The price of bread being the same for all consumers, they all have the same marginal substitutability of bread for all other products. But because the price of bread is below the producers' marginal costs, the marginal transformability of bread into other products is lower than the marginal substitutability, and economic efficiency suffers. The poor do spend a high proportion of their income on bread, and the bread subsidy improves their situation in relation to the more well-to-do. But if they got the same subsidy in cash, they would spend it in a manner that would benefit them more. This is the meaning of damage to economic efficiency.

### Action within the Market

In the case of natural monopolies there are two ways for the government to ensure economic efficiency. One way is to regulate the monopolies; the other way is for the government itself to run the monopoly. Education is another example. It could be entrusted to private institutions with government subsidies, because of the resulting external benefits, but the government could also set up a network of schools by itself.

In addition to public services, such as telephone, electricity, water and gas, and in addition to services yielding external benefits such as health and education, the government can operate in any field whatsoever if it believes that this would increase economic efficiency. In every such instance the objective is not maximum profit but only greater economic efficiency. A government company can enter a monopolized industry in order to make it competitive. But if the government company reaches an agreement with the monopolistic firm so as to increase the profits of both firms, the government company will have failed to achieve the purpose for which it was established.

If a natural monopoly is more efficient when run as a government operation than as a private firm under governmental regulation, the government should run it. But if the private firm is more efficient, and the cost of government regulation is less than the difference in efficiency, then private operation is to be preferred.

The government operates within the market also for its own purposes. The government is a huge organization employing many workers and buying and selling different goods and services. As such, it participates in the market just like any other consumer or producer, but on a tremendously large scale. Here too the government should apply the principles of economic efficiency. It should buy and sell in the market at competitive prices and not exploit its monopolistic and monopsonistic powers. Moreover, it must buy in the cheapest market and itself produce the services it needs if that reduces its costs. Thus, the government must behave like any private firm, choosing the cheapest of the many options, producing the item itself, buying it, accepting the lowest tender for the same quality, subcontracting, and so forth.

But when the government buys goods or services in an imperfect market, it should use the method that maximizes the efficiency of the *economy* even if this does not minimize the cost to the government *company.* It must not exploit its monopolistic and monopsonistic powers to increase its profits, but operate within the framework of the price structure—the given set of prices— meticulously maintaining the equality of the value of marginal product to the value of the marginal factors (which would be the marginal cost if the government enterprise had no monopsony power). Thus the government can play its part, as a consumer and as a producer, to increase economic efficiency by its appropriate participation in the market.

### Action outside the Market
Action outside the market pays no attention to market prices. It is appropriate for public goods and for the large centralized firms, which have already been discussed. In these areas the centralized method is superior to decentralization.

Here the government is confronted with two problems: first, how large the output should be; second, who should be the producer. Since market prices cannot reliably provide a basis for determining size of output, another system of evaluation is required. For example, in order to determine the size of the defense services, research must be conducted into the external benefits from this service and all the alternative outputs that must be given up in order to achieve this output. In order to determine the size and location of an industrial center, research must be conducted into all the effects of these decisions throughout the society.

These problems can be tackled by methods of research and analysis that have been developed in economics, sociology, mathematics and related fields. Complete solutions to such problems cannot be guaranteed, but these research techniques can certainly assist us in approximating overall economic efficiency.

Although decisions of this nature are inescapable responsibilities of government, it is not essential for the government to be the organization that carries them out. Consider, for example, the construction of a dam for flood prevention. The decision is the government's, but construction does not have to be done by a government office. In every situation the task should be assigned to the organization most efficient in the particular task—public or private, centralized or decentralized. In achieving this, the market mechanism can be of help, for example by means of competitive tenders, and by private and public companies on an equal footing.

# Chapter Ten

# Practical Goals and Diversionary Illusions

Up to this point we have been examining the various ways open to a government to achieve its aims, limiting ourselves to specific objectives that can indeed be furthered by the instruments at its disposal. The primary objective sought by a modern welfare economy is that of satisfying the preferences of the consumers, as these are expressed by the choices made by them on a free market. The main specific objectives are price stability, full employment, maintaining the conditions for a competitive market, providing public goods and services and ensuring a satisfactory rate of economic growth.

These objectives are, of course, all helped by economic efficiency. We have looked into the conditions for maximum efficiency and considered how adjustments could be made to correct the market prices for external costs and benefits and governmental preferences superimposed on consumer choices by the use of taxes and subsidies. We have gone into some consideration of measures for correcting, reducing or preventing impairment of economic efficiency by monopolistic restrictions of output, by ignorance, false information and uncertainty. This last concern is of particular importance for growth inasmuch as uncertainty is a powerful deterrent to investment for the future as against using resources for current consumption.

In all this we have considered the equal availability and the equal permissibility of administrative and market mechanisms and how the choice between them, in any instance, should be based solely on whether the one or the other is more efficient in achieving the objective.

But not all government intervention or participation in the economy employs appropriate measures for achieving practical objectives. Much government intervention employs inappropriate measures, often with unexpected and undesirable results. In addition, much governmental intervention is directed at illusory objectives which, when examined more closely, turn out to be meaningless slogans or even hindrances to the achievement of genuinely desirable results.

In this chapter we offer illustrations of misleading concepts that have had a significant effect on economic policymaking in Israel and other countries.

### Planning (To Supplant the Market)

"We need a basic and detailed rational plan which will take the place of the anarchistic market mechanism." This cry is frequently heard. Two arguments are put forward to support it. The first is that free enterprise is unsatisfactory because it serves the profit and the pleasure of the individual at the expense of the public. The second is that private enterprise does not undertake responsibility for tasks that are essential for society and the state, but rather spreads its activities to undesirable areas.

The first argument is based on a moral or ideological attitude of antagonism to the price mechanism. We have shown that the price mechanism is nothing but an instrument for the better satisfaction of the needs of the public. We have also seen that when the conditions for a perfectly competitive market do not obtain, the market allocations will not be efficient, but that even then it makes sense not to discard its use but to correct its imperfections. The ideological approach fails to understand that the market is a *neutral* instrument that makes use of *private interests* for achieving *social objectives.*

The second argument is directed at activities subject to external costs or benefits when the market does lose efficiency, but an adjustment of the price structure can correct this. The proper use of planning is not to destroy the market and inherit its functions, but to make the best use of it, for the closest possible approach to economic efficiency.

### Technical Progress, Productive Efficiency and Capital Accumulation

One of the most widespread confusions in connection with growth and economic development stems from a failure to distinguish between *technological progress* and *capital investment.* There is a twofold reason for this confusion. First is the observed fact that the most technologically advanced countries are very rich in capital. These countries make use of capital-intensive methods, namely, methods that use great quantities of capital relative to the other factors of production, such as land and labor.

A second source of confusion arises from the engineer's approach to production problems. From the point of view of the engineer, technical progress consists of designing the most modern and most refined production instruments, which usually calls for the investment of much capital, that is, for extreme capital intensity.

There is, however, no necessary connection between technical progress and capital intensity. In most cases the different factors of production can be substituted for each other at any given technological level. The economically most efficient degree of capital intensity is attained when the marginal product of each capital good is just equal to its price. Since capital is scarcer in developing countries, its price is relatively high, and in consequence the economically most efficient technology is one with a relatively low capital intensity. This does not mean that a poor country cannot make good use of technical progress. Technical progress does not necessarily mean an increase in capital intensity, but the use of better methods. And improved methods may even use *less* capital (i.e., *reduce* the capital intensity).

There is yet another confusion, that between *technological progress* and an increase in *labor productivity*. Technological progress occurs when better methods permit a larger output to be produced with the same quantities of all the inputs. In this case the increase in output is clearly not due to an increase in capital, but it does not follow that it can properly be called an increase in labor productivity. It is clearly an increase in the efficiency of capital and labor (and any other factor) *taken together*. Nevertheless, such an increase in the ratio of the total output to the quantity of labor (which is the average output per unit of labor) is commonly called "labor productivity" or "labor efficiency," giving labor, as it were, all the credit for the increased output. This is even less appropriate where the increase in the output, or part of it, is due to an increase in the quantity of capital. Since output is always the result of all the factors working together, there is no sense in ascribing all the output to *any* one of the factors.

### Managerial Efficiency of the Firm and Economic Efficiency of the Economy

In general it is customary to see a genuine increase in productivity—more output from the same inputs—as originating within the firm, and to credit it to an increase in managerial efficiency. But this factor must not be considered the only one responsible for the increase, or even the most important one. It is not only within the firm that the factors of production can be made more efficient by better management. The economy as a whole can be made more efficient even if every firm is already using its factors in the most efficient way possible. Efficiency or production can be increased by shifting factors of production from firms where they have a lower marginal product to firms where their marginal product is higher. There will then be an increase in total output without any increase in the input of factors of production and without any change in the efficiency of management in any firm.

### Preference for "More Productive" Industries

Certain industries are often considered by their nature to be "more productive" than others, and are given preferential treatment. Sometimes it is because they produce physical products (heavy industry, and in some cases agriculture) as against the "service industries" (transportation, communications, marketing, tourism and so on). There is no economic basis for this discrimination. Any such preference, by increasing the level of activity in one kind of industry at the expense of another, destroys the equalities required for efficiency.

Such prejudices between different industries, while very widespread, seem to be especially marked in Israel. This may be because immigrants into Israel from countries where it was harder for them to obtain employment in industries like engineering and agriculture tend to be regarded as more valuable because they were less attainable. But there are plenty of precedents for such preferences or prejudices as between different industries. They arise mostly from a misunderstanding of distinctions made for quite other reasons.

Indeed, Adam Smith himself, the father of modern economics, called service industries "unproductive." But all he meant was that they did not produce physical items that could be stored and thus added to the capital accumulation that would contribute to the growth of the wealth of nations. But he was careful to point out that "unproductive" services were often more important than "productive" goods. The Physiocrats, writing in France just before Adam Smith, might have seemed to say that agriculture was more important than other occupations, but what they really said was that land is the only factor that "produced" anything, while other industries only "changed the form" of what comes from the land. Their purpose was to encourage the taxation of land rather than of industry because (as we have seen in Chapter 9) such taxation does less damage to the efficiency of the economy. It was certainly not their intent to discourage industry in favor of agriculture.

### Prestige Products

From time to time the demand crops up for the development in the economy of *basic* or *heavy industry* such as steel or mining, as if the future of the economy depended on such products. This demand is also based on an economic illusion. A "basic" industry, just like any other, is worth developing only up to the point where the price of the product is equal to the marginal social cost. The belief that heavy industry is especially good for a country seems to be based on the same error as the preference for more highly capitalized methods. Countries that were blessed with abundant resources suitable for heavy industry became rich, in part, because of these natural advantages. They did not have to depart from the principles of economic efficiency to develop them. Indeed, it was precisely these principles—of equalizing the marginal transformabilities and substitutabilities—that led those countries to the concentration on the heavy industries. A country that is not automatically pushed in that direction by the principles of economic efficiency can go there only by *departing* from the principles and *reducing* efficiency.

### "Economic Independence"

One source of governmental intervention that is only partially flawed by illusion, or confusion, is the concern about a lack of "economic independence." By this is usually meant the failure of a country to earn by its exports all the foreign currency it needs to purchase its imports. The difference, termed a "deficit on current account of the balance of payments," must be financed by "outside aid" either in the form of foreign loans or gifts.

Some of this concern comes from a simple failure to recognize that if a country is obtaining some outside aid it must inevitably be "suffering" from a deficit in the balance of payments. It would be much more appropriate to say that it is *enjoying* this excess of imports over exports—goods and services which it is getting without having to produce exports in exchange for them. Yet we do find countries complaining about their trade deficit even while they plead for more outside aid. Such complaints might simply be disregarded as unreasonable were it not for the fact that they provide support to claims by exporters for subsidies to export, and to claims by domestic producers for protection in the form of restrictions on competing imports. Both of these would interfere with the price structure required for economic efficiency.

There are, nevertheless, also sound reasons for concern about a continuing import surplus. It involves a continuing accumulation of debt to foreigners that may constitute a very serious future burden of interest payments and capital repayments.

Borrowing makes sense for a country, as for an individual, only if the additional investment it makes possible is expected to yield enough in increased future output to permit the capital to be returned, with the interest, and still leave some remaining benefit for the borrower. And even when this is the case, account has to be taken of whether the increased future output will be saleable for the (foreign) currency required for the repayments to the (foreign) lender. There might still be trouble if expected future outside aid is unexpectedly interrupted so that larger repayments than planned for become necessary.

This kind of trouble has to be considered even in cases where outside aid takes the much more genuine form of gifts or grants of one kind or another. There is then no concern about repayment, but there is still the danger that an interruption of such unexpected aid could cause great difficulty in the adjustments the economy would have to make to the discontinuance of the expected import surplus.

But such risks are by no means peculiar to the needs of "economic independence." The same risk applies to income from exports if there is a possibility of the demand for the export falling off or the ability to produce it being impaired. For a country that depends on one or a very few export industries to earn the foreign currency to pay for vital imports, this danger could be much more serious than the danger of foreign aid drying up. Only if the aid is in the form of loans, and the total accumulated debt grows faster than the GNP, would there be any obvious need for concern. But in any case it is important to recognize that a deficit in the balance of payments is only the reflection (or shadow) of outside aid; it is impossible to have an excess of imports over exports without receiving outside aid.

While the goal of "economic independence" is not a complete mis-conception, other "slogans" with regard to foreign trade and foreign exchange are totally misleading. Some of these are explored below.

### Foreign Exchange

There are a number of illusions connected with imports and exports and the foreign currencies which have to be used in buying and selling them. The foreign exchange rate is a price which, just like any other price, serves economic efficiency when it is equal to the marginal cost. Here the relevant marginal cost is that of the goods that have to be produced to earn a unit of the foreign cur-rency. Many troubles and inefficiencies arise from the aspiration to have one's own national currency valued more highly. This, of course, means somehow keeping down the (domestic) price of the foreign currency. The price of foreign currencies might be kept down by a foreign exchange control. The demand would then be greater than the supply and some kind of rationing would be required to determine who gets how much of it. In this case, clearly, the price is not a genuine price.

When foreign aid is available, it actually provides the additional foreign currency required to satisfy the excess of the demand (by importers who need it to pay for imports) over the supply (by exporters who got it in payment for exports). An import surplus then emerges with the problem of "economic dependence" we have already discussed. In this case the price of foreign exchange is *genuine,* as long as there is no limit on how much one can buy or sell at the official price. But it is not *correct,* because the calculations of the importers and the exporters do not take into account the social or external marginal cost of the continuing depletion of foreign reserves or the continual increase in the foreign debt of the country.

### Preference for Domestically Produced Goods

"Buy American" in America, or "Buy British" in Britain, are popular slogans. Those who promote them may believe that a preference for domestic products will stimulate the development of the economy and ensure full employ-ment. But what they have uppermost in mind is decreasing the foreign competi-tion with their import-competing products. Accordingly, when mere persuasion fails, they propose *legal* restrictions on the competing imports.

### Export or Die!

Exactly the same arguments have exactly the same questionable validity when claiming superiority for export industries and calling for export subsidies. Sometimes the propaganda takes the dramatic form of our heading. What is true is that such a subsidy-induced shift from producing goods for the domestic market to producing for export has the same effect on the balance of payments as a protection-induced shift from buying imports to buying domestically produced goods. Either one increases an export surplus or decreases an import surplus, in the first case by expanding exports and in the other case by reducing imports.

The effects on the efficiency of the economy are also similar. In both cases industries are unduly expanded. In the one case it is the export industries, and in the other case it is the import-competing industries. The import-competing industries, equating marginal private cost with price, will bring the price above the marginal social cost, which is the lower cost of the alternative foregone, the cheaper but excluded imports that the consumers would have been able to buy in the absence of the restrictions on the competing imports. A subsidy to exports brings the price received for the exports into equality with the marginal private costs of the exporters, but this is below the marginal social cost, which includes the subsidy. In both cases the price is below the marginal social cost. In both cases production is carried beyond the optimum point where price is equal to marginal social cost. The efficiency of the economy as a whole is lessened by an over-expansion of the export industries or the import-competing industries.

This objection may not apply to goods that the economy can produce efficiently compared with other countries, but which are held in lower esteem than the foreign goods. The local product needs time to demonstrate its qualities. An investment in advertisement to educate the consumers is in order and could constitute an externality calling for government subsidization.

The argument for supporting import-competing or export industries sometimes takes the form of suggesting that there are external benefits to the economy in the reduction of the trade deficit, and that these externalities justify the intervention. There are here no external benefits in the normal sense, but there is some validity to the argument where the currency is overvalued (i.e., the price of a foreign currency is being kept artificially low). In such a case the expansion of exports (by a subsidy) and of import-substitutes (by a tax on the competing imports) may actually *increase* the efficiency of the economy as much as they would if there were indeed external social benefits.

These interventions may be conceived of as a roundabout way to correct the unduly low price of foreign currency. They make a unit of foreign currency earned more valuable to the exporter (because of the subsidy he gets) and more expensive for the importer (because of the tax he has to pay). This restores the equality of price to marginal cost that had been upset by the artificial lowering of the price of foreign currency. In all such cases it would, of course, be much simpler to permit the "genuine" and "correct" price of foreign currency to be reached on a free market for foreign exchange. But where, for good or bad reasons, it is not possible to have "freely floating exchange rates" (which is the jargon for allowing the market mechanism to operate in this field), the roundabout correction would be better than nothing.

Such a roundabout correction of the price of foreign exchange would call for the subsidy to exports to be equal to the tax on imports, since the undervaluation of foreign currency affects imports and exports equally. Unfortunately this is rarely done. In most cases much more support is given to the import-competing industries than to the export industries, so that a new distortion is imposed on the price mechanism. The nature of the damage from this distortion can be seen especially clearly. If there is a 30 percent tax on imports (which is equivalent to a 30 percent subsidy to the import-competing industry) and a 10 percent subsidy to exports, the economy is paying three times as much to the import-competing industry as it is paying to the export industry for each extra unit of foreign exchange saved or earned.

In terms of the waste of resources it means that at the margin, 130 units of domestic resources would be used by the import-competing industry to earn the same foreign exchange for which the export industry would take only 110 units.

Where the import restriction takes the form of a quota, the damage can be far greater. Thus, in Israel, there have been cases where import-substitution by the import-competing industry took three or four times as much of the resources to save a dollar's worth of foreign currency as it would have taken to produce the additional exports to earn that extra dollar.

It has been claimed that industries producing physical goods are more prone to become export industries, as if that were a reason for favoring them. This is not necessarily so, as is shown by the tourist industry. In the shrinking and increasingly interdependent modern world, technological progress in travel, transportation and communication services are becoming as mobile as goods, and the distinction between product and service industries loses all significance.

### Conclusion

All the departures from economic efficiency as a result of the illusionary and diversionary slogans have a doubly harmful effect on growth. In the first place, the induced inefficiency reduces total output. Furthermore, the reduction in total output brings with it a *more than proportional* reduction in saving and investment. This is true not only for *voluntary* saving and investment but also for any *forced* saving that can be imposed on the population by taxing or otherwise restricting consumption to divert resources to investment.

This concludes our survey of the principles of efficient economic policy for progress and growth and of some of the main misconceptions that tend to distort it. In the second part of the book we shall turn to the practical problems in the application of these efficiency principles, including the resistances and misconceptions. We shall do this by observing the actual policy carried out in Israel, and its results. Before going into this examination we will present some background information on Israel and a sketch of its general development over the quarter century of its existence.

# Part II

# Economic Policy in Israel

## Chapter Eleven

# Israel: The Economic Background

The general principles of efficiency and growth as applied to Israel will now be examined. We begin with a brief review of the main economic developments in Israel during its first 25 years as an independent state, followed by a chapter summarizing her development in facts and figures.

The rapid growth of the Israeli economy since the establishment of the state is one of the most outstanding phenomena on the world economic scene since World War II. From a relatively backward, underdeveloped economy, with a per capita income of $580 in 1950, by 1972 she had reached a per capita income of $1330 (both measured in 1955 dollars). During this same period the population increased more than three and one-half times, from 900,000 to 3.2 million, while the real gross national product increased eight times. In the course of this rapid economic development, houses were constructed to meet the needs of a massive immigration, new towns were built, new agricultural settlements were established, a modern agricultural system was developed, industry was modernized, a national system of roads was constructed, trade and financial systems were expanded and modernized and a whole new infrastructure for the economy and society was built. At the same time education and health systems were broadened, and government aid programs for low-income groups were introduced. All this was done while a large proportion of the country's total economic resources had to be allocated to defense.

This growth was indeed made possible by a vast capital import that greatly expanded the total resources of the economy, but the progress is still mightily impressive. It is hard to find another case that matches the rate of sustained growth of the Israeli economy over so long a period. However, one should not overlook the fact that this achievement was accompanied by a variety of problems for which there were no easy solutions and which, in fact, called for an efficient and consistent economic policy.

### 1948-1953: Mass Immigration and Austerity

The state of Isarel was established in May 1948, in the throes of a
war precipitated by Arab armies that had invaded the area a few days earlier. All
the economic resources of the small Jewish community (some 650,000 people)
had to be directed to the military effort. The war itself lasted a few months, but
the armistice agreements were not signed until 1949. At that time the process
of rebuilding and settling the country and developing the economy was already
underway, and all efforts had to be mobilized to meet the mounting economic
difficulties.

In 1949 the economic problems of the new state were forbidding.
The gates of the country had been opened during the 1948 war to the Jewish
refugees from Europe. Over 100,000 newcomers arrived in 1948, and about
240,000 in 1949. This mass immigration continued until the end of 1951,
totaling some 700,000 immigrants in three and one-half years. The main problems faced by the economy were how to provide the newcomers with food and
shelter and absorb them into the economy in productive employment. The
economy had to provide a higher rate of consumption, a higher level of housing
construction and a higher volume of investment in agriculture, industry and the
infrastructure. This called for much greater resources than could be provided by
the national domestic product even after it had been restored to its prewar level.
The underdeveloped tax system was inadequate, the budget was in heavy deficit,
and there was a desperate demand for imports to fill the gap.

The government did succeed in achieving at least one of its goals, the
provision of basic consumption to all, including the new immigrants. It achieved
this by a policy of administrative intervention in a regime of austerity, rationing
and price control. Other goals were achieved to a much lesser extent. Unemployment was widespread, and the temporary housing provided for the newcomers
was shockingly inadequate. The difficulties kept piling up. By the end of 1951 the
economy reached a danger point: tremendous inflationary pressures threatened
to turn the supressed inflation into an uncontrolled galloping inflation; black
markets were growing in almost every product; unemployment was severe; there
was a shortage of even the shockingly inadequate temporary shelter; and foreign
exchange reserves were completely exhausted.

Under these conditions the government was forced to adopt a new
economic policy. This included the gradual cancellation of all rationing; a closing
of the inflationary gap by rapid increases of controlled prices; devaluation of the
Israeli pound (while fixing different exchange rates for various products according to their relative urgency); attempts to curtail the rate of increase of the
money supply; and a balancing of the government budget—putting an end to
the inflationary deficit financing. As a result of these measures and a drop in the
level of immigration, the inflation receded and the balance-of-payments deficit was reduced. But this was achieved only at the cost of a reduction in the level

of investment, a slowdown in the rate of economic growth, a decline in construction and an increase in unemployment.

Toward the end of 1953 the economy attained a measure of normalization. At the same time, new sources of capital input were opened up and opportunities were created to expand economic activity by accelerating development efforts. The year 1954 saw the beginning of a period of rapid and sustained economic growth, which continued without interruption to the end of 1965. During these twelve years the real rate of growth was between 10 and 12 percent per annum.

### 1954-1965: Sustained Growth

The 12-year period of continuous growth was by no means a routine one. At the beginning of the period there was severe structural unemployment resulting primarily from lack of adjustment between the capabilities of the employees and employment opportunities. A process of education—training and retraining—accompanied by investment in creating new jobs, gradually reduced unemployment. This decline in unemployment continued without interruption despite the renewal of immigration in 1955 to about fifty thousand newcomers per year.

Throughout this period there were three main lines of development. In agriculture there was a concentration on utilizing all the available land and water in the country—water being brought from the North all the way to the dry areas in the South. Industrial development resumed at high speed in the second half of the 1950s. A concentration on housing construction, especially with government financing, made possible the elimination by 1965 of most of the shocking "transition camps," and most of the newcomers were provided with new housing (much of which was still overcrowded and uncomfortable).

This process of development was accompanied by a policy of population dispersion, mainly to the South, the North and the East—away from the central Tel Aviv area. Some fifteen new development towns in which public housing was built and industry developed were established. However, these development towns remained a weak link in the economic chain, with the structural unemployment primarily concentrated in them.

Another difficulty that arose at the beginning of this period was an increase in tension along the borders with the neighboring Arab countries, which led to the Sinai War in 1956. The resulting burden on the economy of a much higher level of defense expenditure caused a temporary increase in inflationary pressure and in the balance-of-payments deficit.

Following the Sinai War, military activity was somewhat reduced. The inflationary pressures declined, the balance of payments deficit decreased slightly and stability was improved. In the early 1960s inflationary pressures revived and caused an increase in the balance-of-payments deficit. This was still a period of rapid and sustained economic growth, but now it was accompanied by a faster increase in the standard of living, primarily in private consumption. The government tried to improve economic efficiency by cancellation of many of the controls and restraints and by setting up a unified rate of exchange, following a devaluation of the currency in 1962. However (due to factors that will be discussed in later chapters of this book), this goal was not achieved. Instead, the inflation and the balance-of-payments deficit worsened. Indeed, the deficit in the balance-of-payments increased from $350 million in 1959 to $520 million in 1964. Forecasts indicated that were this trend to continue to the end of the 1960s, the deficit would reach a level the economy could not bear. The government consequently decided to embark upon a deflationary policy, deliberately reducing both public and private expenditures.

### 1966–1967: Recession

The deflationary policy embarked on by the government in 1964 consisted primarily of a reduction in government expenditure on investment and housing. A coinciding decline in immigration in 1965 accentuated the policy of economic restraint. As a result, by the middle of 1966 the Israeli economy found itself in a severe recession. Building and construction declined sharply, total investment was reduced by more than 40 percent, unemployment appeared and spread quickly, and economic growth stopped. Prices, which had been rising for some years at an average rate of 7 percent per annum, continued to rise in 1966. The deficit in the balance-of-payments, however, declined from $570 million to $450 million.

In the beginning of 1967 unemployment reached an unacceptable level. The government began to take effective action to encourage economic activity, primarily by advancing development and infrastructural programs. The first steps had just been taken when in June the Six Day War broke out. This war changed not only the map of Israel, but the whole course of its economic development as well.

### 1967–1973: A Period of Development and Inflation

Following the Six Day War, defense expenditures rose sharply, reaching a peak in 1970 of 25 percent of the total domestic national product. Investment also increased very rapidly, part of it directed to the development of modern industry for military products. Unemployment declined rapidly, and by 1969, had completely disappeared. Aggregate demand increased along three lines: expenditures for defense and development; greater consumption at a higher standard of living; and a revival of immigration in 1969. The economy resumed its growth, though at a somewhat slower pace than in the past, namely at 8 to 9 percent per year. The opening of the borders with the administered territories of the West Bank and the Gaza strip did not have an immediate effect on the Israel economy, since the total domestic product of these territories amounted to less than 10 percent of the Israel domestic product. However, during these years an increasing number of the inhabitants of the territories came to work in Israel, and by 1971 they constituted 5 percent of the Israeli total labor force.

The increase in government expenditure was accompanied by a rise in taxation, but expenditure grew at a greater rate and the government resorted to deficit financing on a large scale. The combined increase in aggregate spending from all sources, including the return to full employment and the increased consumption out of increased earnings in economic prosperity, showed itself first in a vast increase in the balance-of-payments deficit. This deficit reached magnitudes never imagined before—over $1 billion. In 1970, prices again began to rise more rapidly, at a rate not known since the early 1950s. This rise in prices was accompanied by a parallel increase in money wages. In the beginning of the 1970s the immediate defense needs were somewhat relaxed, but this coincided with increasing social conflict and tension. The government found it impossible to avoid increasing expenditure on public services, primarily to provide the restive low-income groups with more housing, education, health services and other forms of more direct help.

### The 1973 War and its Economic Outcomes
In 1973 the Israeli economy was enjoying full employment and continuous growth, but was suffering from serious inflationary pressures that were reflected by a high rate of price increase (over 20 percent), a high rate of wage increase, and increasing deficit in the balance-of-payments (above $1.5 billion) and a rapid rise in the country's foreign debt. As the country faced these serious economic problems the 1973 War broke out and caused a sharp deterioration in economic conditions.

Following the war defense expenditures more than doubled, reaching almost 40 percent of the GNP in 1974. Economic growth was stopped, due to the high rate of mobilization of the labor force for military service. Inflation became stronger as the price level increased at a rate greater than 30 percent per year. Taxation increased, and the standard of living declined. But the most serious outcome was the sharp increase in the balance-of-payments deficit (to some $3.5 billion in 1974), which constituted about 40 percent of the Israeli GNP. Without substantial foreign aid, the economy could not function properly.

Facing this grave economic situation it thus became clear that more than ever the economy needed an efficient economic policy to be able to cope successfully with its difficult and dangerous economic problems.

# Chapter Twelve

# Outline of Israel's Economic Development

In this chapter we shall summarize briefly the process of development of the Israeli economy during the years 1950 to 1973. This summary is designed to provide the reader with the background required to follow our review and evaluation of Israel's economic policy, to which the rest of the book is devoted. Accordingly, we shall first review the rate of growth of the real domestic product and then look at the real factors that contributed to its growth: the increase of population and labor force; the accumulation of capital, including the capital import; and the increase in productivity. We shall then examine the main uses of the domestic product and the import surplus—the total resources available to the economy—and look at the industrial components of the domestic product and the general composition of imports and exports. We shall also consider the division of the total resources among private consumption, public consumption and capital formation. We will then examine briefly the inflationary process that persisted during this period. In the last part of the chapter we shall discuss briefly the two main instruments for directing and affecting the development of the economy, namely, the government budget and the monetary system.[a]

### The Growth of Domestic Output

Rapid and sustained growth of total domestic output was the most important feature in the Israeli economy after the establishment of the state in 1948. The annual average rate of increase of the real domestic product was 10.5 percent. There were only two years, 1966–1967, in which growth was stopped and recession persisted. Table 12-1 shows the development of the domestic

[a]A detailed description of the development of the Israeli economy and its growth is in N. Halevi and Klinov-Malal, *The Economic Development of Israel* (New York: Praeger, 1968). The book methodically and very broadly covers the years 1950 to 1965. For later years, a comprehensive, but not concise, account is given in the *Annual Reports* of the Bank of Israel.

Table 12-1.   Real Gross Domestic Product, 1950-1973

|  | GDP (IL millions of 1955) | GDP (Index, 1955 = 100) |
|---|---|---|
| 1950 | 970 | 54 |
| 1955 | 1810 | 100 |
| 1960 | 2860 | 158 |
| 1965 | 4610 | 255 |
| 1970 | 6790 | 376 |
| 1973 | 8730 | 483 |
| 1973:1950 |  |  |

Source: 1950–1965; A.L. Gaathon, *Economic Productivity in Israel,* Praeger (New York, 1971); 1970: *Statistical Abstract of Israel, 1971,* Central Bureau of Statistics (Jerusalem, 1971), p. 155; 1973: Bank of Israel, *Annual Report 1973* (Jerusalem, 1974), p. 16.

national product (DNP) in the years 1950–1972.[b] Table 12-1 shows that during the period reviewed the total GDP in real terms increased 9 times. The annual rate of growth shows a slight trend downward, from over 12 percent in the early 1950s to below 9 percent in the early 1970s. Even the latter rate is impressive.

The rapid increase of the GDP is explained by three main factors: (1) the increase in population and employment; (2) capital accumulation; and (3) increased productivity. Let us now survey the development of each of these factors.

**Population and Employment.**   At the time of its founding in May 1948, there were in the area of the state some 650,000 Jews and an estimated similar number of non-Jews, primarily Arab citizens of Palestine. Following the 1948 War of Independence there remained in Israel only about 160,000 non-Jews. There was a mass immigration of Jews in the years 1948 to 1951 so that by the end of 1950 there were some 1.2 million Jews and 170,000 non-Jews. Table 12-2 shows the growth of the Israeli population and labor force from 1950 to 1973.

From 1950 to 1973 the number of citizens of Israel increased 2.4 times, or 6 percent per annum. This rapid increase resulted from the mass influx of Jews and the high birth-rate of non-Jews. The number of Jews increased in this period by about 1.6 million, of whom 1 million were newcomers. The number of non-Jews increased rapidly due to natural increase at an annual average rate of 4 percent (one of the highest in the world), and the annexation of East Jerusalem. With the population growth there was a similar increase in the labor force (see Table 12-2).

During the years 1948–1950, the main source of immigration was

[b]In order to save space in this chapter we present statistical data for each fifth year only, from 1950 to 1970 and for 1973. Detailed annual data can be found in the sources mentioned in the preceding footnote.

**Table 12-2. The Population and the Labor Force—1950-1973**

| | *(thousands)* | | | | *Civilian Labor Force* | |
| | *Total* | *Jews* | *Non-Jews* | *Total (Index, 1955 = 100)* | *Labor Force (thousands)* | *Labor Force (Index: 1955 = 100)* |
|---|---|---|---|---|---|---|
| 1950 | 1,370 | 1,203 | 167 | 76.6 | 450 | 72.7 |
| 1955 | 1,789 | 1,590 | 199 | 100.0 | 619 | 100.0 |
| 1960 | 2,150 | 1,911 | 239 | 120.2 | 736 | 118.9 |
| 1965 | 2,598 | 2,299 | 299 | 145.2 | 912 | 147.3 |
| 1970 | 3,001 | 2,561 | 440* | 167.7 | 1,001 | 161.7 |
| 1973 | 3,307 | 2,810 | 497 | 184.8 | 1,118 | 180.6 |

*Including some 70,000 residents of Eastern Jerusalem, which was annexed by Israel in 1967.

Source: *Statistical Abstracts of Israel,* Central Bureau of Statistics, Jerusalem.

Europe. From 1951 on, the majority of the immigrants came from the Middle East and North Africa. In 1969 there was a reversal, with the majority of immigrants coming from Western countries and the Soviet Union.

The population structure, as indicated by "continent of origin" of the family head, has gone through dramatic changes. In 1972, 47 percent of the Jewish family heads were of Asian and African origin, 44 percent originated in European and American countries and 9 percent in Israel. The population as a whole, however, had a different distribution: 25 percent were born in Africa and Asia, 27 percent in Europe and America, and 47 percent in Israel.

The skills and abilities of Israel's labor force, both Jewish and non-Jewish, improved significantly over the period as a result of intensive educational activity. With the establishment of the state of Israel, 8 years of free and compulsory education was instituted. In 1969 this was extended to 9 years. High school attendance increased rapidly and the number of students in universities and colleges increased from 1,500 in 1950 to about 50,000 in 1973.

As a result of these developments there was an impressive increase in the level of education of the labor force. In 1963, for example, 45 percent of the labor force had 9 or more years of schooling; by 1971, the figure had reached 54 percent. The percentage of employees with higher education (from 13 years and up) increased during this period from 12 to 17 percent. The percentage of illiterates (primarily newcomers from Oriental countries) declined from 10 percent in 1963 to 5 percent in 1971.

**Capital Formation.** The second factor responsible for the rapid growth of the Israeli economy is the accumulation of capital. The increase in the fixed productive capital stock and buildings (including housing) is shown in Table 12-3.

During the years 1950-1972 the capital stock in real terms increased more than 12 times, and capital per employee increased over 5 times.

**Table 12-3.   Gross Fixed Capital Stock, 1950–1972**

|      | Total Capital Stock | | Capital Stock per Employee | |
|------|---------------------|------------------------|----------------------------|----------------------|
|      | *IL million of 1955* | *Index: 1955 = 100* | *IL Thousands of 1955* | *Index: 1955 = 100* |
| 1950 | 2,150  | 45  | 4,800  | 62  |
| 1955 | 4,780  | 100 | 7,700  | 100 |
| 1960 | 8,120  | 170 | 11,000 | 143 |
| 1965 | 13,570 | 284 | 14,900 | 194 |
| 1970 | 22,600 | 473 | 22,500 | 292 |
| 1972 | 27,200 | 569 | 24,300 | 316 |

Source: Figures for 1950–1965: Gaathon, op. cit, p. 228, and author's calculations; for 1970–1972: Bank of Israel, Research Department (estimates).

A high and continuous rate of capital-formation persisted over most of the years under review. During the years 1950–1955, total capital formation amounted to 25 percent of the gross domestic product. In the next 10 years, 1956–1965, it was 22 percent of the GDP. From 1966 to 1970, it declined to an average of 14 percent per year. In 1971–1973 it increased again to above 25 percent of the GDP. This capital-formation was financed not by a high level of saving but rather by the high flow of capital import. The households and the business sectors did, indeed, save part of their income (between 5 and 7 percent), but the government absorbed most of these savings in its budget deficits. As a result, total savings of the domestic economy in most years was negative. It follows that almost all of the capital-formation came out of capital imports.

The high flow of capital imports made it possible to increase the import surplus (the excess of total imports over total exports in the form of the so-called deficit on current account of the balance-of-payments). This import surplus was financed from different sources, as shows in Table 12-4.

From Table 12-4 we learn that total capital imports to Israel in the years 1950–1973 was $2 billion greater than the import surplus. This balance was accumulated in the form of foreign exchange reserves. About two-thirds of the capital imports consisted of grants and unilateral transfers. The most important of these was the transfer of capital by Jewish institutions. Second in importance were the restitution payments by the government of West Germany. Reparations paid to the Israeli government were a most important source during the years 1953–1964. Grants from the U.S. government were high in the early 1950s and became the most important factor as of 1973.

Among long-term loans, the most important were the State of Israel Bonds. These long-term loans were at relatively low interest rates. In most cases holders of the bonds renewed them automatically. Another source of long-term loans, of increasing importance at the beginning of the 1970s, was the U.S. government, which provided long-term credit for the purchase of military equipment. The rest of the foreign debt consisted mainly of commercial loans at rela-

**Table 12-4. Import Surplus and Capital Import, 1950–1973 (millions of dollars)**

| | 1950–1955 | 1956–1960 | 1961–1965 | 1966–1970 | 1971–1973 | Total |
|---|---|---|---|---|---|---|
| Import Surplus | 1740 | 1670 | 2260 | 3800 | 4940 | 14,410 |
| Total Capital Import | 1630 | 1690 | 2880 | 3730 | 6430 | 16,360 |
| Unilateral Transfers | 1080 | 1350 | 1740 | 2420 | 4000 | 10,590 |
| Compensation from Germany | 210 | 370 | 200 | – | – | 780 |
| Reparations from Germany | 20 | 300 | 630 | 710 | 780 | 2,440 |
| Jewish Contribution | 490 | 360 | 440 | 1040 | 970 | 3,300 |
| U.S. Government | 210 | 70 | 40 } | | | |
| Other | 150 | 250 | 430 } | 670 | 2250 | 4,070 |
| Long-Term Capital | 530 | 400 | 1070 | 1530 | 2300 | 5,830 |
| State of Israel Bonds | 200 | 190 | 150 | 460 | 720 | 1,720 |
| U.S. Government | 330 | 120 | 200 | 490 | 680 | 1,490 |
| Other Loans and Investments | – | 90 | 720 | 580 | 900 | 2,620 |
| Short-Term Loans | 20 | –60 | 70 | –220 | 130 | –60 |

Source: *Statistical Abstracts* and Bank of Israel *Annual Reports*.

Table 12-5.  The Sources of Growth of the GDP:
1950-1969* (percent)

| | | Sources | | |
|---|---|---|---|---|
| | *Growth of GDP* | *Labor* | *Capital* | *Productivity* |
| 1950–1969 | 10.5 | 2.8 | 3.3 | 4.4 |
| 1950–1955 | 11.9 | 3.8 | 3.5 | 4.6 |
| 1955–1960 | 10.6 | 3.0 | 3.3 | 4.3 |
| 1960–1965 | 10.7 | 3.0 | 3.8 | 3.9 |
| 1965–1969 | 8.1 | 1.1 | 2.2 | 4.8 |

*Excluding housing.
Source: Gaathon op. cit., pp. 152–193.

tively high interest rates of 5 to 10 years duration. The total balance of foreign debt at the end of 1973 was $5 billion. This outstanding debt is a potential source of future difficulties, both commercial and political. Further increases in imports, which will require an increase in such loans, may bring substantial risks to the economy.

**Increased Productivity.**  To these two sources of growth—increases in the labor force and in the capital stock—one must add a third: increasing productivity. This is a result of many influences. Among them are the rise in the level of education, the increased skills of the labor force, the increase in managerial efficiency, the introduction of more advanced technologies and the improvement in the operation of the economy as a whole, i.e., the increase in economic efficiency.

In the years 1950 to 1969 the average annual rate of increase of the gross domestic product, excluding housing, was 10.5 percent. During this period the labor input increased by 3.82 percent per annum, and the capital input by 11.37 percent. The contribution of the increase in the labor force to total output or GDP (excluding housing) was 2.8 percent (which is 27.2 percent of the growth), while that of capital amounted to 3.3 percent of the total output (37 percent of the growth). The balance of the increased GDP (excluding housing), 4.4 percent (i.e. 42 percent of the growth), is due to productivity increase.[c] Table 12-5 shows the data in greater detail.

The data on the overall GDP, including housing (which is available only for the period 1956-1965), is somewhat different. While the total annual rate of growth reached 11 percent, the contribution of productivity amounted to only 2.9 percent (i.e., 26 percent of the growth). On the basis of this data we

[c]The above figures refer to the domestic product, excluding housing. For the economy, including housing, there exist data only up to 1965. For details, see Gaathon, *op. cit.*

estimate the contribution of increasing productivity to the growth of the GDP for the whole period 1950-1969 at 33-35 percent.

### The Composition of the Product and of the Employment

During the period under review the Israel economy underwent structural changes in the composition of the gross domestic product (see Table 12-6).

In the first decade, agriculture had a high priority and indeed grew very rapidly. However, as full utilization of land and water resources was reached at the end of the 1950s, its rate of growth slowed down. The low-income elasticity of demand for agricultural and food products constituted a second reason for this slowdown. The increase in productivity reduced the required input of labor. Whereas in 1955 agriculture provided 15 percent of all employment, its share gradually declined, and in 1973 it provided only 7 percent.

In the beginning of the 1950s manufacturing industry did not receive the highest development priority, but since the mid-1950s it has been receiving a greater share of development investment. Accordingly, the share of the manufacturing industry increased both in relation to the GDP and in total employment, the latter rising from 24 percent in 1954 to 29 percent in 1973.

Construction was more subject to fluctuation over this period than any other industry. The importance of financial services increased, while that of trade services relatively declined. The share of government and nonprofit organizations in the GDP and in employment remained fairly stable.

### Foreign Trade

One of the characteristics of the Israeli economy is the relatively high volume of foreign trade. The total value of imports in 1973 reached over $5 billion, more than 60 percent of the GDP, and throughout the years there has

**Table 12-6.   Industrial Structure of the Net Domestic Product, 1952-1973 (percentage at factor cost)**

|  | *1952* | *1955* | *1960* | *1965* | *1970* | *1973* |
|---|---|---|---|---|---|---|
| Agriculture | 11.4 | 11.3 | 11.7 | 8.5 | 6.4 | 5.8 |
| Manufacturing | 21.7 | 22.5 | 23.8 | 24.2 | 24.2 | 26.2 |
| Construction | 9.2 | 8.4 | 7.2 | 7.2 | 9.5 | 10.7 |
| Transportation & Public Utilities | 9.4 | 9.1 | 10.3 | 10.8 | 10.8 | 12.3 |
| Trade & Finance | 25.2 | 23.3 | 22.4 | 23.1 | 23.0 | 21.5 |
| Government & Nonprofit Organizations | 18.2 | 20.0 | 18.7 | 18.7 | 19.4 | 17.1 |
| Ownership of Dwellings | 5.2 | 5.4 | 5.9 | 7.5 | 6.7 | 6.4 |
| Total GDP | 100.0 | 100.0 | 100.0 | 100.0 | 100.0 | 100.0 |

Source: *Statistical Abstracts* and Bank of Israel *Annual Reports.*

**Table 12-7.   Imports and Exports of Goods & Services (millions)**

|         | 1950 | 1955 | 1960 | 1965 | 1970 | 1973 |
|---------|------|------|------|------|------|------|
| Imports | 300  | 427  | 670  | 1280 | 2630 | 5200 |
| Exports | 60   | 140  | 340  | 710  | 1290 | 2640 |
| Deficit | 240  |      | 330  | 570  | 1360 | 2560 |

been a persistent growth in foreign trade (see Table 12-7). Despite the impressive increase in exports, the excess of imports over exports increased very rapidly, especially after 1967 and again in 1973.

There were also changes in the composition of imports and exports. The proportion of consumption goods in imports declined, while that of raw material increased. There was also a substantial increase in the proportion of military defense equipment, particularly after the Six Day War and again after the 1973 War.

Of the increase in exports, an outstanding proportion was due to manufacturing industry, especially diamonds and textiles. The proportion of agriculture declined (despite an absolute rise). Of significant importance were the increases in transportation services (shipment of oil, air travel) and other tourist services.

### Total Resources and Their Main Uses

The total resources of the economy consist of the domestic product and the import surplus, as shown in Table 12-8. At the beginning of the period, the proportion of import surplus in the total resources was relatively high, above

**Table 12-8.   Total Resources and their Uses: 1950-1973 (percent)**

|      | Total Domestic Resources (National Income) | Resources | | Uses | | |
|------|------|------|------|------|------|------|
|      |      | GDP | Import Surplus | Private Consumption | Public Consumption | Gross Capital Formation |
| 1950 | 100.0 | 79.5 | 20.5 | 59.2 | 16.0 | 24.8 |
| 1955 | 100.0 | 78.7 | 21.3 | 58.2 | 15.8 | 26.0 |
| 1960 | 100.0 | 84.9 | 15.1 | 60.2 | 16.1 | 23.7 |
| 1965 | 100.0 | 83.5 | 16.5 | 58.6 | 17.9 | 23.5 |
| 1967 | 100.0 | 87.1 | 12.9 | 59.1 | 26.1 | 14.8 |
| 1968 | 100.0 | 84.4 | 15.6 | 55.7 | 25.0 | 19.3 |
| 1969 | 100.0 | 81.7 | 18.3 | 53.7 | 25.1 | 21.2 |
| 1970 | 100.0 | 79.8 | 20.2 | 49.6 | 28.6 | 21.8 |
| 1971 | 100.0 | 81.4 | 18.6 | 48.5 | 27.3 | 24.2 |
| 1972 | 100.0 | 81.8 | 18.2 | 47.9 | 25.7 | 26.4 |
| 1973 | 100.0 | 72.9 | 27.1 | 42.6 | 32.2 | 25.2 |

Source: 1950-1965, W. Halevi and R. Klinov-Malal, op. cit., p. 94; 1967-1971: *Statistical Abstract*, 1972, p. 154; 1972-1973: Bank of Israel *Annual Report*, 1973.

20 percent, which means that the import surplus constituted more than 25 percent of the GDP. This high rate prevailed until the middle 1950s. With the stabilization of the economy and the growth of its product, the ratio declined, from 22.5 percent in 1956 to 18.2 percent in 1957 to 15.1 percent in 1960. After a small rise in the early 1960s it declined to a minimum of 12.5 percent during the 1966 recession. After the Six Day War the dependence of the economy on foreign aid rose once again, with the proportion of import surplus increasing to about 20 percent in the early 1970s. After the 1973 War it sharply jumped, reaching 50 percent of the GDP in 1974.

The main uses of the resources are in private consumption, public consumption and investment. We have already seen that the economy directed a relatively high proportion of its resources to capital formation. Table 12–8 shows that this rate was highest at the beginning of the 1950s and then declined gradually. It declined drastically during the recession of 1966–1967 but soon recovered.

With the increase in real national income there was also an increase in the level of private consumption. In order to decrease the dependence of the economy on import surplus, without impairing capital-formation and growth, economic policy was aimed at reducing the proportion of private consumption. Table 12–8 shows that this policy was not successful up to 1967, as the share of private consumption in the use of total resources remained between 58 and 60 percent. However, after 1967 the burden of taxation increased, and as a result the share of private consumption declined substantially. In 1972 it reached a rate of 48 percent. With the increase in the balance-of-payments deficit for defense expenditure, it further declined to 42 percent in 1973. In 1974 it declined further.

In the 1950s public consumption absorbed between 15 and 16 percent of the total resources (excluding 1956, in which defense expenditures rose due to the Sinai War). From the beginning of the 1960s there was a slight upward trend, reaching 17.9 percent in 1965. In the recession of 1966–1967 the ratio of public consumption was deliberately increased by the government. After the Six Day Way, with the rapid increase in the import surplus, there was also a substantial increase in public consumption primarily for defense, bringing its share from 17.9 percent in 1965 to 26 percent in 1967 and to 36 percent in 1970. Later it declined to 29 percent in 1972. In 1973 and in 1974, it rose again reflecting the increased defense expenditures following the 1973 war.

### Prices

Inflation prevailed in the economy during most of the period under review. At the beginning of the 1950s the government suppressed the inflation. With the suspension of controls as from the end of 1951, prices increased rapidly and continued to rise until the end of 1954. In the middle of the 1950s inflationary pressures were still quite strong, but after the Sinai War of 1956 they diminished and relative price stabilization persisted until the end of 1959. In 1960, inflationary pressures increased again and the rate of price increase rose to an annual average of 7 to 8 percent. Even in 1966, when there was widespread unemployment, prices increased as a result of delayed wage increases. The 1966 inflation was a cost inflation, while in the earlier years, and in the years that followed, the inflation resulted from excess aggregate demand.

Towards the end of the recession the price level stabilized and remained stable, despite the resumption of full employment in 1968 and 1969. However rapidly increasing aggregate demand finally ended the stabilization and brought about a price rise, starting in 1970, at an annual rate of 12 percent. This rate increased further in 1973 and 1974, resulting mainly from a more rapid increase of aggregate demand, and partly from a worldwide rise in the prices of commodities and energy.

The inflationary process was accompanied by a series of devaluations. When Israel was established in 1948, the Israeli pound was linked to the British pound sterling at a 1:1 ratio. Devaluation of the pound sterling in 1949 led to a subsequent devaluation of the Israeli pound to IL 0.36 to the dollar. In 1952 two other exchange rates were set in addition to the official rate of IL 0.36; these were IL 0.71 to the dollar and IL 1.00 to the dollar. Import and export products were classified and assigned one or the other of these exchange rates. Such a system of multiple exchange rates ruled until mid-1955. In April 1953 a fourth rate was set, IL 1.80 to the dollar. In December 1953 the two lowest rates were abolished and the rate of IL 1.00 to the dollar became official. However, the main method of increasing the effective exchange rate during this period was the shift of products from lower to higher exchange rates. In July 1955 the stepwise devaluation was completed and a new single official exchange rate was set at IL 1.80 to the dollar. This rate remained in effect until February 1962, when it was increased to IL 3.00. In November 1967, following the 1967 devaluation of the pound sterling, the rate was set at IL 3.50 to the dollar. In August 1971, when the rate of exchange of the dollar was allowed to float, the Israeli pound was again devaluated, to IL 4.20 to the dollar, and has since remained tied to the dollar. In 1974, further devaluation brought the rate to IL 6.00 to the dollar.

### Government Operations

Many of the developments of the Israeli economy surveyed above were powerfully influenced by the government. The government gets its economic strength from its direct control over a large share of the total resources of the economy. It mobilizes and acquires the greater part of the capital import and raises internal resources in taxes and loans. The government also exercises influence by its expenditures of all kinds and by the laws and regulations it enacts, such as its control of foreign exchange transactions, prices and elements of the capital market.

In the early 1950s external resources constituted about 30 percent of the government's income. Its share then declined gradually, falling to 15–18 percent in the 1960s. After the Six Day War, however, its share again increased, to about 30 percent. In most years government income from taxes was between 50 to 60 percent of its total income.

Government expenditure on public consumption was always relatively high. In the 1950s and up to the mid-1960s it constituted some 16 to 18 percent of the GDP. Following the Six Day War of 1967 it increased to over 30 percent, reaching a peak of 35.8 percent in 1970. The main component of public consumption was always defense. In the 1950s this constituted some 8 percent of GDP (except for 1956, when it reached 14 percent), and in the early 1960s some 9 to 10 percent. Defense expenditures rose sharply after the Six Day War, reaching a peak of 25 percent in 1970, declining from that peak to about 20 percent in 1972. In 1973 it increased sharply and in 1974 it reached a level of about 35 percent of the GDP.

Other public consumption items are education, health, welfare, culture, religion and so on. In addition the government allocates part of its budget to investment, either directly or by providing loans to investors, primarily through a development budget.

Up to the end of the 1960s taxes of all kinds came to 25 percent of the GDP. This is surprisingly low compared to most Western European countries, where they were between 27 and 37 percent. Only from the end of the 1960s were the tax rates increased substantially, bringing the total income from taxes in 1972 to about 37 percent of the GDP (with an additional 34 percent in compulsory loans). In 1973 it further increased to 39 percent (43 percent including compulsory loans) and in 1974 the total taxes and loans reached about 46 percent of the GDP, becoming among the highest in the world.

### The Monetary System

The monetary system includes the central bank (the Bank of Israel) and commercial banks. This system creates the money supply for the economy. Three main factors that determine the volume of this money supply are the conversion of foreign to local currency, loans to the government by the Bank of Israel and the commercial banks, and commercial bank credit to the public.

During most of the period under review the total money supply rose at a high rate, and this was one of the main reasons for the inflation. The rate of increase was particularly high at the beginning of the 1950s (30 percent per annum). From then until the mid-1960s it was between 10 and 20 percent per annum. After the Six Day War this rate of increase was accelerated, and in 1971–1973 it increased by about 30 percent per annum (1972—32 percent).

The main item in this rapid increase of the money supply was government borrowing from the banking system to finance its budgetary deficits. It was especially high at the beginning of the 1950s, in 1956 (the Sinai War), in the recession period, and after the Six Day War.

Second in importance was the increase in bank credit to the public. This increase was reflected in the increase in economic activity.

Third was the conversion of foreign exchange. There were years in which the balance of foreign exchange reserves went down. This tended to reduce the money supply and, in fact, partly checked the increase. During years in which foreign exchange reserves increased, the banks paid out Israeli pounds for the foreign exchange, thus increasing the domestic money supply. Such expansionary effects were notable from 1958 to 1964 and especially in 1971–1972. On the other hand, in the first years following the Six Day War, the economy lost foreign exchange reserves and this offset most of the expansionary effect of the government deficits.

### Summary

The Israeli economy has been very dynamic, characterized by a rapid rate of population increase, a high level of capital import and an impressive speed-of-output growth, resulting in a rapidly increasing standard of living. A special burden on the economy has been defense expenditure, which increased much faster than the rate of output growth. The high rate of investment combined with the increasing level of defense expenditures was made possible, despite the low level of aggregate savings, by a rising burden of taxation combined with an increasing import surplus. This latter made the economy increasingly dependent on foreign aid.

During most of this period the economy enjoyed full employment but suffered from almost persistent inflation. The economy passed through a process of modernization that increased managerial efficiency, and thereby increased productivity, as well.

The Israeli government has been deeply involved in economic activity, having a substantial influence in all its main spheres. It is for this reason that an efficient economic policy can play a crucial role in Israel's economic development. We turn now to examine in detail how economic policy was determined, what impact it had and what lessons can be learned from the Israeli experience on how government policy can be used to improve the efficiency of an economy.

## Chapter Thirteen

# Foreign Trade

Foreign trade policy determines the economic relations between countries. The most decisive factor in foreign trade policy is the *effective* rate of exchange. The *official* exchange rate is the price in Israeli pounds of a unit of foreign currency. There are, of course, exchange rates for every foreign currency, but it is convenient and customary to use the U.S. dollar to represent them all. A higher rate of exchange thus means a lower value for the domestic currency unit in terms of the foreign currency unit.

The government sets the effective rate of exchange in two steps. First, it sets the official exchange rate, at which residents can buy and sell foreign currency. Second, the government sets tariffs on imports and premiums on exports. An importer of goods from the United States, for example, can purchase the necessary dollars at the official exchange rate, but when these products reach Israel he will pay a tax in accordance with the tariff rate. This tax is equivalent to an additional payment for the dollars already bought from the government to pay for the imports. The effective exchange rate for imports thus consists of the official rate plus the import tax.

The same applies to Israeli exporters. When they exchange the earned foreign currency for Israeli pounds, they receive both the official exchange rate and an additional payment as an export premium. The effective exchange rate for exports thus consists of the official rate plus the premium payment.

The effective rate of exchange determines the cost of imports in local currency. It also establishes the price of exports in the foreign currency. The effective exchange rate thus determines which local products and industries can actually compete with foreign products both in Israel and abroad. It thereby influences the size of the deficit in the balance-of-payments. At a lower rate there will be more imports, fewer exports, and vice versa. The effective exchange rate is thus a strategic economic factor.

### The Effective Exchange Rates:
### 1950-1962

As recounted in Chapter 12, the official exchange rate of the Israeli pound gradually increased from IL 0.36 per dollar in 1949 to IL 3.00 in 1962 and IL 4.20 per dollar since 1971. Most of the time there was only one official exchange rate in force, but during the period 1952-1955 a multirate system operated. However, in all these years there were, in fact, many different *effective* exchange rates. These rates resulted from various arrangements, such as export premiums and import levies, both direct and indirect, which in different periods were set at different rates for different industries and products. We will briefly survey six such arrangements in effect before 1962.[1]

### Taxes and Levies on Imports

Taxes and levies on imports raise the effective rate of exchange and make imported products more expensive, so that less is imported, thus reducing the deficit in the balance-of-payments. Often the tariff is imposed to protect local producers from foreign competition. Income for the government is also a major consideration. In early 1956, with the relaxing of import quotas, the effective exchange rate on imports became an important factor in considering new tariffs and other import levies. The average tariff rate during this period in which the official rate of exchange was IL 1.80 to the dollar, increased from IL 0.23 per dollar's worth of imports in 1956 to IL 0.65 in 1961.[2] These tariffs, however, were imposed at different rates on different types of products, deliberately discriminating between imports according to the purpose for which they were used. While the overall average import levy was IL 0.65, the average tariff on investment goods was IL 0.30, whereas on consumer goods it reached IL 1.70. Within these different groups there were also significant differences: on food products, for example, the average tariff was IL 2.70, while on some other consumer products the rate was only IL 0.60.[3]

### Export Premiums

Premiums—to encourage exports—were first granted in 1950. Until 1956 the premiums were a subsidiary measure that operated along with other more important mechanisms. From the beginning of 1956 until the 1962 devaluation, such premiums were the principal means of increasing the effective exchange rate for exports. These premiums were calculated on the basis of the "net foreign exchange earned" by the exported products, or the "foreign exchange value added."[a]

---

[a]In production both local and imported raw materials and factors of production are used. The added value represents the value in the final product of the local factors and raw materials. The value of the imported production factors and raw material is the "import content." Only the excess of the foreign currency attained over the import content constitutes "net foreign exchange earned," or "foreign exchange value added."

Officially, all industrial exports were to receive a uniform premium, which, in 1955, reach IL 0.85. However, throughout this period, special premiums were also granted to specific branches and enterprises. The disparity in premiums increased from 1959 on. For citrus exports, and for export of diamonds and of services, special premiums of IL 0.36 were set—at a rate lower than that on industrial exports. For specific industrial branches (such as textiles), premiums were set especially high, at IL 1.20. With the 1962 devaluation, this method of granting premiums on exports based on foreign exchange added-value was abolished.

### Foreign Currency Deposits

Under this system, first introduced in 1953 and continued until 1959, the exporter was permitted to use part of his foreign currency receipts for buying otherwise restricted imports. As the exporter could sell these imported goods in Israel at relatively high prices, he received an additional profit that would compensate him for losses on exports. As a result the effective exchange rate varied from one industry to another, depending on differences in the fraction of the foreign currency earnings allowed as "foreign currency deposits." In 1959, with the official exchange rate at IL 1.80, the average effective exchange rate for foreign currency deposits was estimated at IL 3.04.[4]

### Bilateral Trade Agreements (Clearing)

The price levels on imports and exports were higher in countries with controlled foreign currency than in countries where no such control existed. To offset this distortion the government deducted a certain rate (*disagio*) from the foreign exchange receipts on exports to countries with foreign currency control, and granted premiums (*agio*) on imports from those very countries. In general, the disagio rate was equal for all exporters; however, the agio rate was set at a specific level for each transaction and varied from time to time. These arrangements reached their peak in the years 1953–1954, declining thereafter. Toward the end of the end of the 1950s the system was abolished.

### "Imports without Payment"

Imports without payment were those imports that did not require a foreign currency allocation from the government.[b] The importer was permitted to acquire foreign currency from any sources available to him and use it to purchase imported goods. However, he was required to sell to the government at the official rate a sum of dollars equal to the value of his imports. Under this arrangement, again, there were different effective exchange rates. For building material, for example, the effective exchange rate in 1951 was estimated at between IL 1.50 and IL 2.20.[5]

[b]This scheme was mainly in use during 1949–1952, a period in which the black market in foreign currencies flourished in Europe.

### Cartels and Equalization Funds

Cartels and equalization funds, an arrangement that was introduced
in several industries at the end of the 1950s, operates as follows. The industry
is organized as a cartel and receives legal approval under the Business Restrictions Law. The cartel raises the price of the product on the local market and
collects from member firms a certain percentage for an equalization fund. The
proceeds are used to subsidize export of the same product. This is equivalent
to a subsidization of exports by means of an indirect tax on local sales of the
product. The higher local price has to be protected from foreign competition
by import restriction. Such arrangements were introduced, for example, in the
textile and plywood industries, the effective exchange rate varying from industry to industry.

### The Effective Exchange Rates:
### 1962–1973

The declared objective of the devaluation of February 1962 was
to replace the different exchange rates with a single, effective rate. The official
exchange rate was increased from IL 1.80 to the dollar to IL 3.00 to the dollar,
an increase of 67 percent. However, in terms of the previous *effective* exchange
rates, the actual rate of devaluation was much lower, and different for each
industry. Imports of consumer goods had an effective devaluation of 17 percent compared with 54 percent for imported investment goods. For industrial
exports the effective devaluation was only 10 percent. In order to have the
same effective exchange rate for imports as for exports, a gradual reduction
of the high protective tariff was planned.

Equalization of the effective exchange rates was designed to correct
the distortions in the allocation of resources in the economy by the unequal
effective exchange rates. With this plan the government publicly demonstrated
its proper understanding of the role of the price mechanism in achieving economic efficiency. But in the end the plan did not work out.

In the years following the 1962 devaluation, with the rise of the
price level, tariffs on imports were raised, retaining in fact their pre-devaluation
discriminations. Thus the average tariff rate in 1965 was IL 4.50 on imported
consumer products, IL 1.70 on investment goods and IL 1.30 on raw materials.[6] The program for reducing the protective tariffs was fought by the industrialists, and when finally put into operation, was ineffective. In spite of
price increases, no export premiums were granted. Instead the system of cartels
and equalization funds was revived. Another method of encouraging export
was also introduced: subsidization of costs of production factors, principally
the interest on working capital of export industries. In 1966 the subsidization
of exports was extended to include rebates on National Insurance payments
and other taxes. This policy, again, generated different effective exchange rates
on exports. Up to 1969, no further changes were made in the effective exchange

rates. In 1970 the tariff rates were increased and export incentives widened. The policy of multiple effective exchange rates continued, even though there was a minor reduction in the differences. This was brought about by a 20 percent levy on all imports and a 20 percent premium for all exports, introduced in August 1970, and by the devaluation of August 1971. By the end of 1971, the average effective exchange rate was IL 7.60 for imported consumer products, IL 5.30 for raw materials and IL 5.50 for investment goods. At the same time the effective exchange rate for industrial exports averaged IL 5.30, for agricultural exports IL 5.20 and for the export of services slightly above the official exchange rate of IL 4.20 to the dollar.[7] In 1972 and 1973, with the increasing inflation, both the tariff rate on imports and the export premiums were gradually increased, raising thereby the effective exchange rates. This process continued in 1974. In November 1974, when there was a further devaluation to IL 6.00: $1.00, tariffs and premiums were adjusted to fix the effective exchange rate at about 7.00 to 7.50 Israeli Pounds to the dollar.

### Evaluation of Foreign Trade Policy

A survey of the exchange rates clearly shows that throughout the period under review the effective exchange rates for imports and exports were higher than the official rate. We have seen (Chapter 10) that a system of tariffs on all imports and premiums for all exports, both at the same rate, is similar to a devaluation at that rate. But in spite of this apparent similarity there is a difference.

Foreign transactions involving the transfer of money not connected with the import or export of goods are not affected by the tariffs and subsidies. Such transactions are international loans and the transfer of capital for investment purposes. These capital transfer transactions are carried out at the *official* rate. We thus find that a tariff and premium system, at equal rates, results in two effective exchange rates. In Israel, during most of the period reviewed, the effective exchange rate for capital transactions was the official one, while the effective exchange rates for imports and exports were higher.

Moreover, throughout this entire period there were differences between the effective exchange rates for imports and for exports; and there were also differences within each of these two groups for different import and export products.

Most of the time there was discrimination against exports and in favor of import substitutes, as premium rates given to exports were lower than the tariff rates levied on imports to protect local manufacturers. Most seriously discriminated against were the export of cirtrus fruits, diamonds and services, industries that enjoy relative advantages and could withstand the low effective exchange rates. Agriculture, and some branches of manufacturing, benefited from especially high effective exchange rates. The effective exchange rates for imported consumer products was higher than for investment goods and raw materials.

A discriminatory effective exchange rate policy wastes resources by creating different rates of transformation of local resources into foreign currency. Suppose the effective exchange rate for diamond exports is IL 5 per dollar, and that of radio equipment imports is IL 7. In this case, IL 7 worth of local resources are used up at the margin in producing local radios to save the dollar that could have been earned by IL 5 worth of resources devoted to processing more diamonds.

A common argument is that the important thing is to save dollars rather than local resources. But the local resources saved can be used to earn or save additional dollars. Behind the argument that it is more important to save dollars probably lies an intuitive feeling that the official price of the dollar (that is, the exchange rate) is too low. The excess of imports over exports means that more dollars are needed to pay for the imports than are earned by the exports. This, seen as an excess of demand for dollars over the supply, appears as a scarcity of dollars and creates the feeling that the dollar is worth more than the official exchange rate in pounds. As we have seen, the import surplus is the inevitable accompaniment of foreign aid on capital imports.

We thus have a contradiction between the declared policy and the actual policy. When the government announced its New Economic Policy in February 1962, it said:

> The abolition of the multiple rates and the introduction of a single rate is now a fact . . . The single rate has removed the distortions which had an unfavorable influence on economic development in the last period.[8]

Nevertheless, multiple, discriminatory effective exchange rates have remained in force. In February 1962 the government announced its policy of "exposure" (of domestic industry to foreign competition) by gradual reduction of protective tariffs on import substitutes. This was done very slowly. The average effective rate of exchange for a dollar saved, (that is, the effective rate of exchange for competing imports) was IL 6.9 in 1962. It was indeed cut down in 1963 but rose to IL 8.2 in 1964 and in 1967 it reached IL 10.7.[9] The publicized decisions to accelerate the process, which were made every now and then, were only partly executed. On the other hand, the government opposed the granting of premiums on exports, which would have reduced the gap between the effective exchange rate for exports and the higher protective effective exchange rates for domestic production. Its view was expressed in the following words:

> It is not our intention to provide export premiums. Granting such

premiums means choosing the easy way out; it means postponing
the facing of the realities in the world markets, not to mention
the budgetary problems involved.[10]

Instead of granting premiums directly to export, the government initiated (in
1966) a method called "export incentives."[11]

In both cases, however, the exporter is subsidized. The only difference
between "premiums" and "incentives" is that the premium system would have
made possible a single effective exchange rate for exports and imports, while
the incentive method results in multiple effective exchange rates. For example,
one of the export incentives introduced in 1966 provides tax rebates of 1 percent of the overall export value on export of products with up to 25 percent
added value. When the added value is 26–45 percent, the tax rebate is 3.5 percent and reaches 6 percent at 46–65 percent added value, and 8 percent when
the added value exceeds 66 percent. Under this arrangement the premium
fluctuates from IL 0.14 to over IL 0.50 per dollar of value added.

It is difficult to understand why, after the 1962 policy of unifying
the effective exchange rates was declared, there was a return to the policy of
multiple rates. The government may have wanted to prevent the enrichment
of producers in certain industries (those able to produce at a lower exchange
rate) and to support other industries (those unable to produce at a low exchange
rate). But measures intended to increase equality of income should be separated
from those designed to increase economic efficiency. There are more efficient
ways of increasing equality of income.[12]

By the end of the 1960s the government apparently had become
aware of the harm resulting from these policies. From 1970 onward the government began to take measures to reduce the spread of the effective rates of
exchange. The principle of "premiums" for exports was accepted, and the
premiums (no longer "incentives") were increased at the beginning of 1970.
In August 1970 there was a levy of 20 percent on all imports, together with
premiums of the same percentage on a significant portion of exports. The devaluation of August 1971 brought the effective exchange rates a little closer to
each other. However, very little has so far been done to unify the exchange
rates. The policy declaration of 1962 was not yet realized by the end of 1974.

## NOTES

1. A description of these arrangements is found in M. Michaeli, *Foreign Trade
   and Capital Imports in Israel* (Am Oved, Tel Aviv, 1963). See also D.
   Pines, *Direct Export Premiums in Israel* (Falk Inst., Jerusalem), 1930.
2. See Joseph Baruch, "Export Levies and Subsidies in Israel in the Years
   1955–1961," *Bank of Israel Bulletin,* No. 18, November 1962,
   pp. 41–61.

3. Ibid., p. 43
4. Michaeli, op. cit., p. 108.
5. Michaeli, op. cit., p. 108.
6. See P. Davidov, "The Liberalization of Imports—February 1962–May 1965," *Bank of Israel Bulletin,* No. 26, August 1966, pp. 43–57.
7. See V.D. Amiel, "The Effective Exchange Rate in Israeli Foreign Trade, 1962–1971," *Bank of Israel Bulletin,* No. 39, February 1973, pp. 24–46.
8. "Budgetary Law of 1963–1964," *Knesset Minutes,* vol. 35, file 10, 1966, p. 637.
9. E. Tov, "Exposure Policy in Israel from 1962 to 1967," *Bank of Israel Bulletin,* January 1972, pp. 24–44.
10. "Budgetary Law of 1966–1967," *Knesset Minutes,* vol. 44, file 13, 1966, p. 613.
11. "But we will increase the export incentives, and a substantial sum has been allocated to this in the budget presented to you," ibid.
12. See Chapter 20.

# Chapter Fourteen

# Price Regulation and Manipulation

Price regulation and price manipulation have frequently been used by the government for economic objectives. At different times direct price controls were imposed to prevent prices from rising, in the belief that this is an effective method for curbing inflation. The government also manipulates the price structure by taxes and subsidies. The stated purposes of the taxes were financing the government budget, altering the level and the structure of consumption, protecting local industry from competing imports and reducing the deficit in the balance of payments. The purposes of the subsidies are to restrain price increases, thereby delaying increases in the cost-of-living allowances, and to increase income equality.

Another instrument for price manipulation is the Business Restrictions Law. Paradoxically, the government has used this law as a means of encouraging associations and cartels, allowing them to raise prices on the local market to finance the subsidization of their exports.

### Price Control

Price control in Israel was introduced at the beginning of World War II. After the war the control was relaxed, but with the establishment of the state of Israel it was strengthened, and took two principal forms: *direct control,* by setting ceilings on the prices of goods and services; and *indirect control,* through pressure exerted by the government on producers to prevent them from raising the prices of their products. In the years 1949–1951 the direct-control method was extensively applied, whereas in 1962–1966 the indirect method was used. In 1971 a partial direct control was reintroduced and remained in force until the end of 1972.

The rapid rate of immigration, the backwardness of domestic agriculture and the insufficiency of foreign currency resources created shortages in basic commodities in 1949. The government budget deficits brought about

appreciable increases in money income and money supply. Thus, excess inflationary demand was generated, with an upward push on prices. To check the
inflation, price controls were introduced. At first a "freeze" was declared. A
number of essential commodities were declared "under control" and maximum
prices were fixed for them. Naturally, excess demand for these products appeared,
and a rationing system followed. As the control and rationing system developed,
a "calculation" method was introduced. This method allowed prices to be fixed
according to cost calculations made by producers and approved by the authorities, or according to calculations prepared by the authorities themselves. Prices
were then fixed by the "cost plus" principle, that is, an agreed profit rate was
added to the approved calculation of costs. During the final stages of control an
experiment was made to introduce a "formula" method. This method linked
the determination of prices to certain indexes.[1]

Direct control required a system of ordinances and regulations,
as well as special administration. Given the market pressures, the administrative measures could be effective only if they had public support. Such support
can generally be mobilized only for a limited period, and only in states of
emergency. Initially the government indeed succeeded in mobilizing public
support, but this gradually waned.

The low official prices of the commodities under direct control left
the population with excess purchasing power. A black market soon developed
on which the same controlled goods were sold at higher prices. As public support faded away neither the controls nor the punishments for violating them
could be effective. The black market grew in importance. The excess purchasing
power shifted to products that were free of direct and indirect controls and
pushed their prices up. These goods and services were not subject to control
because they were considered nonessentials or luxuries. The result was an increase
in imports of these products as well as an increase in the profits of producing
them locally. The policy thus achieved the opposite of its purpose—it resulted
in an increase in the balance-of-payments deficit, it encouraged the development
of industries of lower priority (the luxury goods) and it handicapped the industries supplying essential commodities.

It became clear that the policy was responsible for serious misallo-
cations of resources, and, in 1952, the gradual liquidation of the controls had
begun. By the end of 1954 only isolated traces of the control system remained.

During 1954–1962 price controls were very limited, but after the
1962 devaluation their use again increased. The inflation that followed the
devaluation generated strong pressure for price increases. To restrain these
increases price controls were reinstituted, but this time the indirect method
was employed.

The first step was taken in December 1962, with the creation of
four executive bodies: an Inter-Departmental Price Office was set up; authority
was granted to the regional offices of the Ministry of Commerce and Industry;

a public council was appointed to deal with prices; and regional public committees were established. Producers were required to notify the Price Office in advance and had to obtain its approval before increasing the prices of their products. In contrast to the procedure of 1948-1951, however, there were no laws compelling recourse to the Price Office, and no ordinances or regulations for fixing the prices of selected commodities.

The Price Office derived its power of persuasion over the producers from three sources. One source was the system of taxes, duties, and subsidies. The producer who raised his prices without the consent of the Price Office took the risk that they would recommend a reduction of duties on competitive imports, a tax on his product, or the abolition of the product's subsidy. These methods were also employed for stabilizing the prices of imported goods when affected by international market fluctuations. Thus the price of sugar was subsidized when its international market price increased in 1963, and an increase in the international price of coffee was offset by reducing the import duty.

The second source of power was the Business Restrictions Law. This law gives the Councils on Business Restrictions the authority to permit or prohibit the setting up of associations and cartels for price-fixing and market-sharing. The council can intervene whenever such an agreement has been made, and can require its dissolution.

Finally, the Price Office engaged in mobilizing public support for price stability. Public committees were formed and encouraged citizens to present complaints of price increases

The Price Office had partial success in limiting increases in the prices of industrial products in 1962-1965. This was apparently one of the main factors responsible for the slowing down of industrial development and the overexpansion of services. The serious scarcity of essential commodities could justify the policy of price control and rationing in 1949-1951. However, it is hard to justify the indirect controls of 1962-1965, which merely impaired economic efficiency.

In August 1971, following the devaluation of the Israeli pound, and in view of the renewed inflationary pressures as of 1970, the government reintroduced direct price control, this time by special legislation. The controls were designed to regulate prices of agricultural and industrial products as well as of housing. Again, a Price Office was established, headed by the Price Officer. The Price Office policy was to allow prices to rise only at that rate necessary to compensate for the increased cost of imported raw materials resulting from the devaluation (and later from rising prices in foreign countries).

The controls did not achieve their goals. During the first nine months prices of the controlled products rose between 9 and 16 percent, as compared to the 4-8 percent allowed by the policy guidelines.[2] These increases were not in accordance with the increase of costs or of relative demand, but were the outcome of political compromises and were harmful to economic efficiency.

The smallest price rise was in the manufacturing industry, which had less political influence than agriculture. The decline in the relative prices of industrial products reduced profitability of investment in manufacturing with a greater adverse effect on products with high added value, since compensation for cost increases was granted only for the imported raw materials and not for the local inputs.

Moreover, there were cases in which the controls, paradoxically, pushed prices even higher. For example, before the devaluation there was an excess demand for apartments. The construction firms were able to sell apartments up to two or three years in advance, before handing them over. Because of the controls, these firms decided to hold up their advance sales for a limited time. As a result, the price of second-hand apartments (not covered by the controls) rapidly rose to a much higher level.

Toward the end of 1972, the government realized that its policy was causing more harm than good. The Minister of Commerce and Industry stated:

> We have to abolish controls on industrial prices. These controls
> are temporary and contribute little to the protection of the citizen.
> These controls are inadequate because they have to be applied to
> 17,000 products, and this is totally impossible. . . . If these con-
> trols are not abolished, I predict the collapse of many firms. . . .
> Industries subject to controls will not attract investments.[3]

By the end of 1972 most of the controls were suspended, and the legislation was simply ignored.

If the failure of price controls has indeed taught such a lesson, it will have made some positive contribution. But will this lesson endure and prevent such mistakes from being made again in the future?

### Restrictive Agreements

The Business Restrictions Law, enacted in 1959, gave the government authority to permit or to prohibit restrictive agreements among producers and control over the operation of these agreements. This law served as the instrument by which cartels were organized, sometimes on government initiative, sometimes on the initiative of the producers, in order to serve the objectives of government policy. The main purpose of these organizations was to increase exports. An example is the Cotton Fund, in the textile industry. Organized under the Business Restrictions Law, firms in the textile industry were able to raise their prices on the local market. Consumers were virtually restricted from turning to imported textiles by prohibitively high protective tariffs. Accompanying the price increases were levies on raw materials purchased by local manufacturers, the proceeds going to an "equalization fund" that provided export subsidies. Similar arrangements were made for plywood, oil, cement and tires. Permission for restrictive agreements was also granted to "improve quality, reduce or prevent price increases, increase productivity, and improve marketing technology." [4]

Price-fixing by monopolies or producers' associations damages economic efficiency by restricting output to increase prices and profits. However, this is no reason for prohibiting firms from increasing in size, if this will reduce production costs and improve economic efficiency. If the market is small it is natural for a large firm to find itself in a monopolistic position. To prevent monopolistic pricing policies, many countries have enacted laws that help the government to limit the extent of such damage. The Business Restrictions Law in Israel could have served this purpose. However, it was used not to reduce monopolistic restrictions on output but to encourage monopolistic increases in prices and profits on the domestic market in order to compensate for losses on exports caused by the controlled low official exchange rate. The use of monopolistic profits to subsidize exports can be seen as a way of raising the *effective* exchange rate for exports—to the extent that these profits really were used to subsidize exports.

Encouraging exports by these means is economically inefficient. First of all, changes in the domestic prices of only these particular products disturbs the efficiency of allocation of the production factors. Moreover, this method fixes the effective export exchange rate at a different level for each product. The effective exchange rate for every industry depends on the rate of increase in local prices, on the proportion of local sales to exports and on the percentage of the added value in the exported product. Arrangements of this sort do not encourage export in accordance with the principle of efficiency and impose an unnecessary burden on the economy (see Chapter 13).

## NOTES

1. Details of the control methods introduced in the 1950s appear in Yoram Weiss, "Price Controls in Israel," *Bank of Israel Bulletin,* No. 37, March, 1971.
2. See *Price Controls in the Economy,* International Consultant, 1972, p. 3.
3. As stated in "Ha'aretz," November 26, 1972.
4. *Survey of Ministry of Commerce and Industry, 1964/65* (Jerusalem, March 1966), p. 15.

## Chapter Fifteen

# Factor Prices

Governments often manipulate the prices of factors of production to achieve economic policy objectives. The Israeli government is able to exert a dominant influence over land prices, for example, since most of the available land is under its ownership; the same holds for water and other natural resources. Through laws and regulations it exerts almost complete control over the mobilization and allocation of capital. While there is no direct control over wages, the government's influence can be felt in this sphere, too.

Such controls can distort the price structure so that it does not adequately represent the relative scarcity of the factors.[a] A reduction in the price of a factor of production can encourage producers to increase output, but will also result in extending the use of the cheap factor to activities in which its marginal output is too low. The same objectives can be achieved by means that do not induce this waste. The damage from inefficient methods may well exceed the benefits for the sake of which they are applied.

In this chapter we will survey Israel's factor price policies in relation to capital and credit, water and land. Labor will be considered in Chapter 16.

### Interest-Rate Policy

Capital investment was an essential factor in the economic growth of Israel and in raising the living standards of its citizens. Investors raise their capital from savers either in Israel or outside the country; foreign investors transfer their funds to Israel as grants or loans or by direct investment. The *capital market* is the mechanism that mobilizes capital by transferring it from savers to investors.

[a]It should be kept in mind that the following discussion applies to all factors of production as well as to products used as inputs in the manufacturing of other products (steel, cement, electricity, etc.).

In Israel the government plays a decisive role in the capital market. It controls most of the loans and the unilateral transfers (donations) from abroad. The government also exercises control over the financial investments of the saving institutions, such as provident funds and insurance companies. The government influences the use of private savings through its control over the securities market (stocks and bonds), over the saving programs of banks and other financial institutions and by directing part of the banking credit. As a result the government, directly or indirectly, controls more than two-thirds of the assests of the financial institutions.

The government controls investments both through its development budget and by direct and indirect influence on the operations of the financial institutions. These institutions—such as the industrial development bank and the mortgage banks—raise most of their capital in the domestic and international capital markets, under government control, and allocate this capital to various uses as directed by the government.

The government's power over the capital market is firmly based in the legal system. The Interest Law provides the government with control over official interest rates; the Defense Laws provide the government with control over capital and monetary transactions with foreign countries and over capital issues in the domestic market. Control is also exercised over the domestic market by the Corporations Law. A further influence over capital allocation rests on the Law for Encouraging Capital Investment.

The Interest Law extends governmental authority to the fixing of maximum interest rates. Until 1970 the government regulated both short-term and long-term credits. The interest rate on short-term loans for several industries was set at 11 percent, and for manufacturing industry and agriculture at 10 percent. Long-term loans (for two years or more) were linked either to the cost of living or to the exchange rate. The maximum interest rate on linked loans was 8 percent . On unlinked loans it was 12 percent. In 1970 the regulation of short-term credit was discontinued, but long-term loan regulations remained in force. Within the framework of the Interest Law the government determines disparate rates, depending on the borrower and on the purpose of the loan. Thus, agriculture receives loans on easier terms than industry; firms in development areas are favored over firms in other areas, and export firms are favored over firms producing for the local market.

During the first half of the 1950s unlinked loans for financing investments were provided by the development budget. The inflation made the real interest rate loans negative.[b] With the linking of long-term loans to the consumer price index (as of the second half of the 1950s), the real interest rate became

[b]Assume that a loan of IL 100 was granted for one year at 6 percent interest. By the end of the year, IL 106 must be paid back. If during the year the level of prices rose by 15 percent, the real value of the money repaid is IL 92.20 (IL 106/1.15). The real interest rate is thus minus 7.8 percent (−7.8 percent).

positive. Negative real interest rates reappeared during the sixties when the fund for encouraging exports began operating. This fund provided unlinked loans at 6 percent. During 1962–1965 the price level rose by an average rate of 7.5 percent per annum. The real interest rates on these loans was negative, averaging minus 1.5 percent per annum. In 1970–1972, when the rate of price increase reached 12 percent per annum, the real interest rate declined to about minus 5.5 percent. In 1973 and 1974 this real rate decreased further, to below minus 20 percent.

The purpose of the economic policy in the capital market was to accelerate the rate of economic growth through increased investment; to encourage development of agriculture and industry; to raise the growth rate of the development areas, and to encourage exports. The government sought to achieve these aims by providing especially low interest rates on loans for preferred investments. A decrease in the interest rates for *all* investments would be an efficient way of encouraging investment. It would increase investment in all industries, to the point where the marginal rate of return on investments reached equality with the same lower interest rate, and economic efficiency would be maintained.

But discriminatory interest rates result in unequal marginal returns on different investments, and total output is not maximized—just as in the example in Chapter 1 of different productivity of labor in different vegetable farms. A transfer of investment from a firm adjusted to a 6 percent rate of interest to one adjusted to 16 percent would increase output by 10 percent per annum of the amount so shifted.

Social considerations may justify increased output for selected industries and sectors, and discriminatory low interest rates will lead to such a result. But it will at the same time encourage a wastefully excessive use of capital relative to other factors of production. A direct subsidy based only on the output of a product increases the output without bringing in distortions.

It should be noted, however, that if cheap loans are fixed at an amount less than that used by the enterprise, they do not cause an excessive use of capital. If the investor has to raise the additional capital at the unsubsidized interest rate of the free market he will not use too much of it. The cheap rate on the limited amount is then not at all connected with the amount of capital used. It is, in all respects, equivalent to a lump-sum subsidy to the producer of the selected product, with no strings attached as to what production factors he must use. It will not induce him to use relatively too much capital. On the other hand, it will not induce the firm to increase the output of the desired product. It will increase output only insofar as it induces more firms to enter the industry or dissuade firms from quitting.

The Israeli government does indeed lend at low interest only a part of the capital required for investment programs, but this is not a fixed amount— it is a certain proportion of the capital used. Additional use of capital thus still is made cheaper, though only in part; that is, it is made cheaper only by the extra subsidy on the fraction subsidized. The damage to economic efficiency is thus not prevented—it is only reduced.

Another lending policy of the government applies to investments that turn out to be unsuccessful. In such cases the government frequently increases the loans and lowers the interest change in order to help the investors solve their financial problems. Successful investments naturally do not qualify for such privileges. This, of course, encourages investors to make hasty investment decisions and to take excessive risks.

### Short-Term Credit Policy

Current business operations are generally financed by short-term loans, most of which are provided by commercial banks. The volume of bank credit affects the money supply and thereby the stability of the economy. This is why central banks control the quantity of commercial bank credit. Central banks usually refrain from intervening in the allocation of the credit among the borrowers. This, however, has not been the case in Israel.

**Credit Allocation.** The Bank of Israel controls not only the overall quantity of bank credit but also its allocation, channeling short-term credit at low interest rates to government-preferred uses. Banking institutions are required to deposit with the Bank of Israel between 22 percent and 25 percent of their total deposits, over and above the reserves required for controlling the quantity of credit. The Bank of Israel releases these funds only for loans at low interest rates[c] for preferred objectives: working capital for industry and financing exports. In this way the Bank of Israel determines the specific use of credit, indicating who the recipient of credit is to be. This is often done in coordination with government ministries. The Bank of Israel has officially declared its dissatisfaction with its own policy, as is evident from the following statement:

> Distortions in the price of money due to administrative intervention have never been effective—in any country and especially not with us. Different interest rates, for different types of credits, with exaggerated gaps among them, bring strong pressure for extending cheap credits, encourages transactions in the black market, and causes distortions in the economy. . . .[1]

Nevertheless, the Bank of Israel maintains this discriminatory credit policy.

**Bill Brokerage.** The Bank of Israel was also in charge of controlling the short-term rate of interest within the framework of the Law of Interest. Until 1970 a special regulation set the interest ceiling on short-term credit at 11

---

[c]The banks receive compensation for the low interest rates according to a different arrangement with the Central Bank.

percent. At this rate there was an excess demand for credit. As a result a "free market" developed in Israel in the 1950s, providing for credit transactions at interest rates higher than those allowed by the regulations. At the end of the 1950s these transactions were transferred to the commercial banks, which provided mediation between borrowers and lenders. Lenders received no more than the legal rate of interest, but borrowers also had to pay the bank for two services —brokerage and guarantee. The effective borrowing interest rate was thus considerably above the legal maximum. This arrangement, called "bill brokerage," was not considered illegal, and it did improve the efficiency of credit allocation.

The Bank of Israel was opposed to the development of this market but failed to stop it. It stated that "the expansion of the bill brokerage market should be curbed . . . because of its effects on both the monetary expansion and the security of the banking system." [2] Had the Bank of Israel successfully curbed bill brokerage by commercial banks, these transactions would have continued even less efficiently outside the banking system, as in the "free market" of the 1950s, with still greater damage to economic efficiency in resource allocation. Bill brokerage by commercial banks enabled the Bank of Israel to exercise greater control over the quantity of bank credit than did the "free market" activities. This was achieved by limiting the volume of guarantees the banks were permitted to grant.

In 1970 the ceiling on interest rates for short-term credit was abolished, removing the principal reason for the existence of bill-brokerage. The profitability to the banks was further damaged by the Bank of Israel's imposition of reserve requirements on these guaranteed bills. Thus, during 1970, the volume of bill-brokerage transactions declined and finally merged with regular bank credit, where interest rates rose to an intermediate level between the previous 11 percent ceiling and the level prevailing in the bill-brokerage market. The efficiency of credit allocation also improved. Preferred borrowers, however, who had been obtaining regular bank credit at the Interest Law ceiling, were compensated by an increase in their allocations of directed cheap credit. This development, of course, harmed the efficiency of credit allocation and it even may have more than offset the gain from the abolition of the interest ceiling.

### The Pricing and Allocation of Water

Water is both a consumer product and a factor of production. The same principles of economic efficiency apply to the consumption and production of water as to any other economic activity. Water is not fixed in supply. It can be increased, but only at increasing cost. If the underground water supplies do not suffice, other water sources can be utilized, such as storing flood waters, purifying drainage water and desalinating sea water. As the economy uses increasing quantities of water it must pay an ever-increasing marginal cost for additional water.

One question is: How much water should be supplied? The principle of efficiency requires water to be provided up to the point where its marginal cost is equal to the value of its marginal product. If the marginal cost is greater than the value of the marginal product, the economy is providing too much water. If the marginal cost is less than the value of the marginal product, an increasing water supply would increase the net output of the economy. Moreover, for maximum benefit, water must be allocated throughout the country so as to equalize the value of marginal product of the water in each area to the marginal cost—including the cost of transporting the water to the area. It is thus quite impossible to separate the question of how much water should be supplied from the question of how much should be supplied to each region and for each use.

Water can be allocated efficiently among the different areas and among all its different uses by administrative methods, but only if the authorities have accurate knowledge of the value of the marginal product of water for each area, for each consumer and for every use. Complete knowledge is also required of transportation costs to the various points of use. But water can also be allocated efficiently by the market if each consumer and producer can purchase as much water as he demands at the price set for his region. To achieve his own maximum benefit, each user will adjust his demand so that the value of the marginal product in each use will be equal to the price he pays for it. This method promises greater efficiency because it is enough for the authorities to know only of the cost of supplying water to each region.

The main use of water is for agriculture. The following discussion of water pricing policy will concentrate, therefore, on this industry.

In Israel water prices are set by government authorities. In 1966 the price per cubic meter varied between 2 and 10 agorot (100 agorot = IL 1) depending on the distance from water source to the area supplied. In the North, where water is plentiful, the price per cubic meter was 2-4 ag.; in the South the price was 6.5 ag.; in the mountain regions, 7.5-9.5 ag. per cubic meter was paid.[3] The value of the marginal product of water was estimated at that time at 10-13 ag. in the North and 16-20 ag. in the rest of the country.[4] Studies in some kibbutzim revealed much higher values of marginal product—50 ag. and more. These findings show that the value of marginal product of water differed from region to region and that in every region the price of water was lower than the value of its marginal product. This is why there was great excess demand for water everywhere, requiring rationing of water and the imposition of quotas. Using water in excess of the quota involved the payment of a fine, but water users were prepared to pay the fines, deliberately using water in excess of their quotas, because the value of the marginal product was greater than the price plus the fine.

The quota method, insofar as it is effective in limiting the use of water, is, in fact, a form of administrative allocation. By keeping water prices below the value of marginal product it results in excess demand for water and in pressure from the agricultural sector on the authorities to increase water output. This pressure results in excessive and wasteful investment in increasing the water supply even though the resources applied to this effort could contribute more if used in other ways.

The waste from overinvestment in products for increasing the total supply of water is quite apart from the economic inefficiency of the administrative rationing that must follow from the low price. The excess of the value of the marginal product over the low price will be different in different places, and for different uses. Unless the fines work exactly like higher prices, and the adjusted price-cum-fine is made equal to the marginal cost, there will be different values of the marginal product of water in different uses and regions with a resulting waste, since the water used to produce a lower-valued marginal product could have produced a higher-valued product.

The claim is often made that a low water price is an important condition for achieving desired objectives, such as the settlement of unpopulated development areas and the cultivation of arid land. The economic inefficiency of this method emerges from the following example.

Suppose that in order to encourage agricultural development in the arid land of the South, the government provides a subsidy that reduces the price of water to farmers in the South from 20 ag. to 8 ag. per cubic meter; and assume that this land is then irrigated by 2000 cubic meters of water per acre per annum. The subsidy thus reduces costs by IL 240 per acre. If cultivating this land without the subsidy would result in a loss of IL 80 per acre, cultivation would be discouraged. With the subsidy there is a net yield of IL 160 per acre, and the land is settled and cultivated. Assume that the farmers are growing tomatoes selling at 20 ag. per pound. With water at 20 ag. per cubic meter, the marginal product of water is obviously 1 pound of tomatoes. If the price of water is reduced to 8 ag., it becomes worthwhile not only to cultivate the arid land but also to increase the use of water everywhere. In fact it would be worthwhile to increase the irrigation of tomatoes until the marginal product of a cubic meter of water fell to 0.4 pounds of tomatoes (which is equal to 8 ag. in value). Water would also be substituted for other productive factors, and used for growing other crops, including crops that require such large quantities of water that they are not worth growing when water costs 20 ag. Increasing use of water for these purposes would be at the expense of other uses that have a marginal product value in excess of 8 ag. (and even much above 20 ag.), but where the quantities are limited by the water quotas. Reduced water prices thus indeed extends the cultivation of arid land, but it also encourages wasteful use of water.

It is, however, possible to encourage the agricultural development of arid land without wasting water. One way would be to grant a direct subsidy for each cultivated acre. In our example, a subsidy of IL 240 for each acre of arid land cultivated would immediately provide the same net product of IL 160 per acre. But the settler would find that he could economize on some of the expensive (20 ag.) water by using it more carefully than if it cost only 8 ag., substituting other factors for it. A smaller money subsidy would then be as great an inducement as the larger amount—the IL 240 provided in the form of cheaper water—which he gets only if he uses the full 2000 cubic meters.

Since our purpose is not the greater use of water but rather the settlement of the arid land, it is not surprising that we get better results if we subsidize the settlement of arid land rather than the use of water.

Moreover, if it should turn out that what we really are interested in is not necessarily increasing the cultivated land but increasing the number of settlers in the area, it would be even more efficient to provide a subsidy for each settler rather than for each acre of land cultivated.

These considerations gave rise to the appointment of a committee in 1970,[5] to examine the distortions in water prices throughout the country and to suggest appropriate improvements. In its 1971 report the committee stated that "the use of unrealistic calculation of water costs is not consistent with efficient management of water projects," and thus "it is desirable to establish a direct relation between costs of water and the prices up to a reasonable ceiling," with the purpose of "reducing the distortions which may result from unrealistic calculation of water costs." [6]

The committee recommended a close link between the price of water and the supply costs in each area, but only where the cost is not higher than 35 ag. per cubic meter. This was to be the ceiling price even where costs were higher. The committee also recommended fines of 45 ag. per cubic meter for water consumed over and above the quotas.[7]

The committee opposed full linkage of water prices to water costs, explaining its position as being "in principle, owing to the important functions fulfilled by the agricultural sector in settling the country, increasing its security and encouraging population dispersion.[8] The recommendations were thus a first step in the direction of improving the efficiency of the water allocation system. By compromising between considerations of economic efficiency and the political pressures exerted on the committee, it left room for additional future improvements.

### Land Pricing Policy

Land policy in Israel consists of three elements: (1) determining land prices; (2) designating land uses; and (3) fixing land taxes. In this chapter we will consider only the determination of prices.

In contrast to any other production factor, land is distinguished by its fixed quantity, which cannot be increased. This characteristic has been a decisive factor in the determination of land price policy.

To understand the land pricing policy of the Israel government it is necessary to go back to its origins, which preceded the establishment of the Jewish state. The Jewish Settlement in Palestine undertook as one of its main tasks the acquisition of every possible piece of land, at any price, without considering its possible use or value. The sale of national land was prohibited and the land was leased to settlers throughout the country at symbolic nominal rates unrelated to marginal products. This was a sacred code and found different forms of expression. Here is one of them:

> To increase our possession of the land, at any price and by any means—this is the task which stands before us today. . . . And now there is before us only one problem: the land of Israel is in danger and we must redeem large areas quickly.[9]

With the establishment of the state of Israel, conditions changed abruptly. A sizable amount of Arab land in the center of the country and at the borders, from the South to the North, came under government control. It became clear that for its efficient allocation a pricing policy was necessary, but the government's land policy remained unchanged. The government was unable to free itself from the ideology of the preceding period and thus could not adopt the principles of economic efficiency in the allocation of land.

Up to 1965 there were no policy guidelines. There was only the basic principle that land is not for sale and can only be leased. Agricultural land was leased at a uniform price per family unit, and the price of urban land was fixed administratively.

This tradition persisted through fifteen years of statehood. However, the distortions that accumulated over the years and the skyrocketing of private land prices during the economic boom in the early sixties finally compelled the government to reconsider its land policy and formulate clear guidelines.[d]

Public ownership of land is not, as such, in conflict with efficient economic policies for maximum output from the available productive factors. Even if the sale of land is prohibited and only leasing is permitted, appropriate lease rates could yield economic efficiency. All that is required is that the lease rates be equal to the value of the marginal product. Thus the allocation and use of land need not be affected by its being available only for lease and not for sale; but lease rates and the allocation system have a decisive effect on economic efficiency.

The use of land involves substantial externalities. For example, an industrial area close to a residential area causes harm to the residents; the location of business centers, industry, commerce and entertainment determines the travel time and expenses of both employees and customers.

In order to insure the efficient allocation of land, these external influences must be taken into account. Moreover, managerial efficiency calls for large areas to be set aside for homogeneous uses such as industrial centers, ports,

---

[d]A Committee for Investigating Land Policies in Israel was formed in September 1963. The committee's recommendations were accepted and put into effect in May 1965.

commercial centers and the like. Such allocations cause significant changes in the prices of different pieces of land. Thus it can be assumed that administrative allocation of land, when carried out in accordance with the principles of economic efficiency, will result in greater well-being than that achieved by the price mechanism alone, which does not take appropriate account of the externalities.

Administrative allocation of land is established by master plans. However, after the master plan is set and land allocation by zones for different types of use have been legally approved by official authority, the task of administration is completed. From this point on the competitive market mechanism can best serve to set the appropriate prices that will reflect the value of the marginal product of the units of land for different uses, and will assure economic efficiency in its utilization.

In Israel the method of administrative allocation of land by means of master plans has reached a high level of competence. The national ownership of much of the land facilitated this development. However, the second stage of detailed allocation, which should be based on a competitive market mechanism, has not been sufficiently developed.

**Agricultural Land Price Policy.** The land policy of 1965 distinguished between agricultural and urban land. Agricultural land was to be leased to the agricultural producers and settlers who were to cultivate it. The size of a unit of land per family was to be determined by a proper government authority.

Before 1965 there was a uniform land rent per "family unit." In 1961, for example, the rate of such a lease was IL 41.60 per annum. This method was abolished in 1965, when the lease was set at 2 percent per annum of the net income of the family unit.

On both methods the actual rent payment was lower than the marginal product.[e] The demand for agricultural land was consequently greater than its supply, and administrative allocation of land among the settlers had to be employed.

Economic waste from excessive use of a factor whose price is set too low can occur where the quantity of the factor is not limited. This is not the case with land, since not only the total area of land but the amount of land allocated to each settler is fixed. But administrative allocation of the land is still bound to be inefficient for two other reasons. First, settlers do not have identical capabilities. Thus, for one settler the marginal product of his land may be high, while for his neighbor it is much lower. Because it is impossible to transfer land from one settler to another a potential increase in output is lost. If the price of land were set at the value of its marginal output, the second settler would not be able

---

[e]Studies on the marginal productivity of agricultural land in several agricultural settlements substantiate this finding.

to keep his land for too long; some of the land would be transferred to the first settler, with whom it has a higher marginal product, and total output would be greater. The second reason is that low lease-rates give rise to pressure for larger land allocation for agricultural settlement, taking land away from other uses where the value of the marginal product is greater.

**Urban Land Price Policy.** The 1965 policy stipulated that urban land was also subject to leasing. It allowed, however, for some "exceptions," where the government decided to sell land. In these cases the price was to be determined as follows:

> The value of urban land should be realistic, that is, at the value in a sale by a voluntary seller to a voluntary buyer, as determined by a government assessor.

> In order to prevent random and speculative fluctuations in land prices, the council shall lay down guiding principles for the government assessor, on the recommendations of a special committee.[10]

Thus, while the policy of setting the price of land sold by the public authorities was "as if" based on the market price, the actual transaction prices were not necessarily equal to the market prices. In fact, the administration had the authority to sell land below the market price. And, indeed, the government offices in charge of carrying out this policy maintained that, in principle, it was undesirable to raise land prices.[11] This policy of selling public land at prices below its market value (which reflects the value of its marginal product) resulted in pressures to misallocate land to inefficient uses.

## NOTES

1. "Report on the Increased Means of Payment During the Period Feb. 28, 1963–Sept. 30, 1963," *Bank of Israel Bulletin,* no. 21, February 1964, p. 139.
2. Ibid.
3. Data provided by the Water Commission of the Ministry of Agriculture.
4. These estimates were published by the Faculty of Agriculture, Hebrew University. See D. Yaron, "Water Supply to Israel Agriculture," *Resource Development in Israel* (Hebrew University, Jerusalem, 1965), p. 24.
5. The Committee for Investigating Alternative Legislation for Water Prices in the Country, *Findings and Recommendations* (Ministry of Agriculture, Tel Aviv, August 1971).
6. Ibid., p. 4.
7. Ibid., pp. 17–18.
8. Ibid.

9. From a lecture by M. Ussishkin. See Ussishkin, Granovsky, and Weitz, *Land Redemption, a Political Factor* (Jewish National Fund Head Office, Jerusalem, three lectures, undated, presumably done in the 1930s).

10. Israel Lands Administration, *Report No. 4* (Jerusalem, 1965), p. 26, para. 5(a), and p. 28.

11. The following is a typical expression of this erroneous position of government officials: "High land prices attract capital for investment in land, thus discouraging productive investments. High land prices also increase housing cost thereby increasing the price index and wages resulting in increased production costs. . . . One should not ignore the fact that high land prices constitute an inflationary factor which is in conflict with the policy of price stabilization. . . . All that was said above brings us to the conclusion that settting a maximum limit on the weight of the land in the price of the dwelling units is essential for a policy which is designed to integrate efficiently the planning of land with construction planning and urban planning in general." D. Tanne, "Land as a Factor of Urban Settlement Policy," *Housing and Construction* (Ministry of Housing, January 1965).

# Chapter Sixteen

# Wage Policy

Labor is the main factor of production in the economy, and the principles of efficient allocation naturally apply to this factor no less than to others. The first rule is that the wages of labor must equal the value of labor's marginal product. This rule sets not only the average wage level, but also the wage differentials, according to the different values of the marginal products of the different kinds of labor.

Wages also constitute the principal source of income for the majority of the population. The wage rates thus affect the different incomes of people. The *wage level* also has a significant influence on the *price level*.

In Israel, as in most other countries, wage rates are determined not be free competition but through the negotiations of pressure groups with opposing interests. On the one side are the labor unions, pressing for wage increases. On the other side are the business associations, exerting opposite pressure to hold wages down. The government stands in the middle taking part in wage fixing not by virtue of formal legislation, but by its general authority over economic policy. In practice, the system is more complicated, since most labor unions belong to the Histadrut (the General Federation of Labor), and the same Histadrut is also an owner of enterprises, thus acting as an employer. The government itself also employs a relatively large number of workers. Along with this interrelated system of forces there is another complication, associated with the three main components of wages in Israel: (1) the basic wage; (2) the cost-of-living allowance; and (3) the fringe benefits. Each component is affected by agreements, amendments and modifications that have accumulated over many years.

This complicated system offers no guarantee that the level and structure of wages will fit in with the principles of efficient allocation of the labor force or with policy judgments on social preferences—including those relating to the inequality of incomes.

*111*

**Wage Level**

The demand for labor is determined by the value of its marginal product. If the wage level is too low given the value of the marginal product, there will be an excess demand for labor; if the wage level is too high there will be an excess supply, namely, unemployment.

**Excess Demand for Labor.**   If the aggregate demand on the economy is greater than what the economy can produce, an excess aggregate demand is created, pushing the price level upward. As a result the wage level becomes relatively too low and employers try to increase employment, since this would add to their profits. But if the economy is already producing as much as it is able to there are no more unemployed workers. The employers try to get workers away from each other, and this results in wage increases. The cost of production thus rises. If aggregate demand keeps on increasing, we have a continuous increase both in prices and in wages. This was the situation in Israel from the early 1950s up to 1965, and again from 1969 on.

In spite of repeated declarations that it would take measures to end the excess aggregate demand responsible for the inflation, the government did not make such measures effective. Instead, it resorted to direct intervention in the labor market to prevent wage increases. But the government failed to achieve its purpose, and the reason for this failure is clear: the excess aggregate demand exerted a greater upward pressure on prices and wages than the administrative and political power the government could bring to bear.

Instead of working to reduce the excess demand, the government claimed that the source of the trouble was the *cost-of-living allowance,* which linked wages to prices. During a ten-year period the government made great efforts to eliminate, or at least cut down, the cost-of-living allowance, and indeed some appreciable progress was made. From 1957 to 1966 many changes in the regulations governing the cost-of-living allowance reduced its importance, step by step. But this did nothing to reduce the pressure for price and wage increases resulting from the excess aggregate demand. For every step taken by the government to prevent increases in the cost-of-living allowance it had to give way in the other components of the wage, namely in increases in the basic wages and fringe benefits. In 1964–1965 the average wage increased by 30 percent. This increase was caused mainly by the excess demand following the 1962 devaluation. Thus when the government's attack on the cost-of-living allowance won a "victory," the overall wage increase was one of the highest on record. The effort to eliminate the cost-of-living allowance was an administrative struggle fought on the wrong front.

A similar development took place in the early 1970s. At the end of the 1965–1967 recession, excess demand for labor reappeared. Again, the government tried to prevent wages from rising and even suggested a "package deal": if wages were not raised above a certain level the government would not increase taxes. This was a return to the policy of the pre-recession period. Since taxes were not raised the excess demand was not reduced. Pressure on the market to raise prices and wages persisted. The "package deal" was indeed signed, but the agreement was broken on both sides. Wages did increase and the government did raise the tax rates.

**Excess Supply of Labor.** When aggregate demand in the economy falls, the demand for labor also declines, and the result is unemployment. This development generates pressure to reduce wages. However, labor unions usually prevent such a decline, and if the depression is not too severe, they can even continue to raise wages.

This is what happened in Israel in 1966–1967. In 1965 there had been significant wage increases. Pressure was exerted for additional wage increases in 1966 and 1967. If unemployment had been small these pressures might have borne fruit. However, the severe unemployment prevented significant wage increases (apart from those obtained by powerful workers' pressure groups in vital industries). Moreover, in 1966 prices continued to rise, thus causing some decrease in real wages. In specific sectors where there was a sharp decline in activity (such as in the construction industry) even the nominal wages declined. It was during this period of unemployment that the government realized its first success in curbing wage increases. Cost-of-living allowances were frozen, while basic wages rose less than productivity.

It should be kept in mind that the governments' success was possible only because it was working in conjunction with, and not in opposition to, the market forces. These forces also exerted a downward pressure on wages, through severe unemployment in the economy. And indeed, when unemployment disappeared, the rise of wages was renewed, at rates higher than planned by the government.

### Wage Differentials

Labor is not a homogeneous factor of production. The value of the marginal product of labor depends on its kind and its degree of proficiency. Efficient allocation of labor requires a wage structure in accordance with the differences in the value of the marginal product of the different kinds of labor.

The Israeli government, while intervening in setting the overall average wage level in the economy, as a rule refrained from entering into the issue of wage differentials. This was worked out by the trade unions and the employers' associations. The Histadrut's policy was significantly affected by an egalitarian ideology, a basic objective of the Israeli labor movement from the days prior to the establishment of the Jewish state. This may, perhaps, explain the fact that wage differentials in Israel are lower than in most other countries.

While the differentials are low, there is a tendency for them to increase. This trend began in the mid-1950s and has continued since then, supported by economic forces that surmounted the ideological obstacles. Nevertheless, the wage differentials remained lower than in other countries. Wage differentials that are lower than the differences in the value of the marginal product cause inefficient allocation of the professional labor force. They discourage specialization and the acquisition of higher education. A youngster who devotes many years to acquiring an education expects, among other things, a higher wage or salary. The return on private investment in education is too low.[a] [1] However, this has not significantly discouraged the urge to acquire a higher education. Social status and prestige, together with the expectation that in the future the wage differentials will increase, still constitute powerful incentives for higher education.

It is possible to achieve the social aim of greater income equality in ways that cause less harm to economic efficiency than by manipulating the wage structure. Such ways are connected with government taxation and expenditure policy (see Chapter 21). It is, therefore, in the public's interest to keep ideological considerations from intervening in the determination of wages, and instead to take them into consideration when formulating governmental budget policy.

In the light of this discussion some generally accepted principles of wage policy are seen to be unsatisfactory. The principle of linking wages to output is often presented as a scientific approach to wage-fixing. But linking wages to *output per employee* causes distortions and harms economic efficiency. For one thing, output is not the product of labor alone. Other factors of production are also involved. If total output increases as a result of an increase in capital there is still an increase in "output per worker" ( the *average* product of labor), even though there might be little or no increase in the *marginal* product, or perhaps even a decrease.

Another shortcoming of the slogan linking wages to output is that it is often applied to *all* wage-earners. In general, there are no homogeneous changes in the value of the marginal product in different professions. What is required is different rates of wage change in the various professions rather than an overall fixed change. Linking all wages to national output makes the current wage structure permanent, thus disregarding the differing developments within the various branches of the economy.

Another slogan calls for an increase in the wages of "workers engaged in production," that is, the wages of workers engaged in manufacturing industry and agriculture, as opposed to those employed in the service industries. Behind this demand are ideological concerns, conflicting with economic efficiency

[a]The findings show that investment in higher education is unprofitable financially, bringing less than an 8 percent return, i.e., considerably less than the rate of return on capital in the economy.

considerations. If the value of the marginal product of labor in manufacturing industry and in agriculture were to increase more rapidly than in the service industries, that would be a good reason for increasing wages in the former industries. But if the value of marginal product in the service industries is higher, that is where wages should be higher.

A widely accepted practice, harmful to economic efficiency, is the freezing of differentials in the wage levels of different professional groups. For example, there is a fixed ratio linking nurses' wages to doctors' wages; elementary school teachers' wages to wages of high school teachers; and so forth. However, changes in technology and in relative demand introduce changes in the ratios between the value of the marginal product of specific classes of professionals. Market forces will press for appropriate changes in the wage structure. Such wage changes will offer incentives to workers to seek employment where the value of the marginal product is greater—that is, where they contribute more. Freezing wage differentials disrupts this adjustment process.

## NOTES

1. See R. Klinov-Malul, *The Return on Investment in Education in Israel* (Jerusalem: Falk Institute for Economic Research, 1966).

# Chapter Seventeen

# The Tax System

Taxation provides the government with the means for achieving social and economic objectives. Taxation, however, by creating a gap between price and marginal cost, damages economic efficiency. An efficient tax system is one that enables the objectives to be achieved with minimum damage to economic efficiency.

In this chapter we evaluate the structure of the Israeli tax (and subsidy) system, its efficiency and its contribution to equalization in the distribution of income.

## The Level of Taxation

The Israeli government has undertaken many tasks that call for heavy government spending; on defense, on immigrant absorption and on investment for development. To prevent spending, or total aggregate demand, from becoming excessive, a relatively high rate of taxation is necessary to reduce spending in the private sector. But in fact, until 1967, the tax burden—as a percentage of the gross national product—was not especially high.[1] In 1962 the overall tax level was 27 percent of the GNP, and similar rates existed until 1967, when it was 26 percent. Only after 1967 did the overall tax level increase greatly, reaching over 36 percent (or 41 percent if compulsory loans are included) in 1971 and about 46 percent in 1974.

In some Western European countries during 1963–1965 [2] (when their average real income per capita was about the same as in Israel in the late 1960s), the tax burden as a percentage of the gross national product was more than 37 percent for France and Sweden; 35 percent in West Germany, Norway, and Austria; 33 percent in Holland; 30 percent in Italy; and 29 percent in the United Kingdom, Belgium, and Denmark. Only Switzerland had an especially low rate of 22 percent. (In the United States it was about 24 percent).

In view of these rates, the real tax burden prevailing before 1967 in Israel was surprisingly low. Only after 1967 did it rise significantly above the level that prevailed in some Western European countries. The high level of capital imports is what made the relatively low rates possible.

The composition of taxes in 1971 was as follows: income tax yielded 32 percent of the total tax yield; national insurance 15 percent; customs duties 20 percent; excise taxes 14 percent; gasoline taxes 4 percent; and property taxes 3 percent. Compulsory loans added some 12 percent to the total revenue. The share of direct taxes in total revenues came to about 52 percent.[3]

In the West European countries direct taxes were, in general, much lower. In 1965 the share of income taxation in total revenue was 23 percent in Italy, 37 percent in France, 39 percent in Belgium and 44 percent in Germany. Only in Holland, at 56 percent, was this share higher than in Israel.[4]

While the overall tax burden was not unusually high, the tax rates were very high. Income tax (including compulsory loans) reached a marginal rate of 50 percent on a monthly income of IL 1050 ($260), 60 percent on IL 1300 ($300), 70 percent on IL 2000 ($480) and 80 percent on IL 4000 ($960). Also noteworthy were the high customs duties and excise taxes, reaching 200 percent and sometimes 300 percent on a number of products.

In spite of the very high rates, the tax burden is still comparable to that of the Western European countries. Here we find the principal defect in Israel's tax system: the narrow bases upon which taxes are levied. This is most glaring with regard to the income tax. In 1971 the revenue from income tax was less than 12 percent of the GNP. The explanation is to be found in the long list of incomes eligible for full or partial deductions; special exemptions; allowances and tax credits. Berglas's analysis shows that taxable income in Israel is less than 30 percent of the national income.[5] Indirect taxes are also levied on a short list of goods and services. In 1967 only one-third of the products manufactured in Israel were subject to purchase tax, but these products carried very high tax rates, averaging 45 percent. There are hardly any taxes on services, while only an eighth of the total turnover of services was subject to taxation in 1967.[6]

### The Inefficiency of the Tax System

As we saw in Part I, the more general the tax system, the more efficient it is. The damage to economic efficiency in Israel from the tax system is especially severe because, as just noted, of the narrow bases upon which taxes are levied. Here there is a vicious circle in that the narrower the base the higher must be the tax rate, which in turn intensifies the damage to economic efficiency.

It is difficult to assess the extent of economic damage caused by the high progressive income taxes on the narrow income base.[7] It affects the willingness to work, particularly at the intermediate- and high-income brackets. It also probably affects the allocation of resources, since it encourages people to choose economic activities with relative low tax rates, even if the result is reduced output and pre-tax income. What counts is the higher *net* income. Berglas's attempt to measure the influence of the income tax on the GNP (using 1965 as the base) revealed that an equiproportional increase in the income tax rates for all levels of income would bring about a significant fall in the national product. Thus it was estimated that an increase of 10 percent (which would raise the average tax rate from 12 to 13.2 percent and the marginal rate on the average income from 27 to 29.7 percent) would result in a drop of 0.7 percent in the GNP.[8] This means that for every IL 1.00 increase in revenues, GNP will drop by over IL 0.58, so that net income after taxes would be reduced by IL 1.58.

Direct taxes are not the only taxes that reduce economic efficiency. Indirect taxes and subsidies do so, too. Levying taxes on expenditures causes a rise in prices; granting subsidies causes prices to fall.[a] Taxes and subsidies thus alter the price structure in the economy. As a result of levying a tax on a specific product, both demand for and output of the product decline. This process continues until the excess of the consumer's price over the marginal cost of production equals the size of the tax. Where there is a subsidy, there is a "negative excess"—the marginal cost exceeds the consumer's price. Because this excess is not the same for every product, the economy's efficiency is harmed. The narrower the tax base, and the higher the tax rate on this narrow base, the greater the damage. Some damage of this kind is unavoidable to the degree that taxation is necessary for achieving social purposes, but economic efficiency is not achieved as long as the extent of this damage is not minimized.

If purchase taxes are levied on a relatively small number of products while services are almost completely free of taxes, there will be an excessive production and consumption of services. Though we cannot estimate quantitatively the extent of the damage to efficiency caused by taxes or subsidies, it is possible to single out specific examples. One such example is provided by the taxes levied on petroleum products.[9] The tax on gasoline is much higher than that on diesel oil. This discriminatory tax results in the use of diesel oil instead of gasoline, despite the fact that the former shortens the life-span of the motor, impairs the performance of the vehicle, reduces the comfort of travel and increases pollution. Since the economy pays almost the same price for diesel oil as for gasoline, it is clear that this discriminatory taxation causes unnecessary damage both to the economy and to public welfare.

[a]The change in price will normally be less than the tax or the subsidy. This is because only a part of the tax (the increase in prices paid) works on inducing the buyer to buy less, while the rest of the tax (the reduction in the net price, excluding the tax received by the seller) goes to induce the seller to sell less. Similarly, only a part of the subsidy goes to cheapen the product for the buyer, inducing him to buy more, while the rest goes to sweeten the price received by the seller (including the subsidy), inducing him to provide the additional amount demanded.

The damage caused to the economy by subsidies is basically of the same nature as that caused by indirect taxes. The subsidy provides the producer with a marginal revenue that is higher than the price paid by the consumer. Accordingly, the producer will expand his output to the point where the marginal cost is *higher* than the consumer's price by the amount of the subsidy. The extent of the damage can be seen clearly in certain cases. One subsidy reduced the price of bread to the point where it was cheaper than chickenfeed. Chicken producers responded by feeding bread to their chickens. The whole production process, from grinding the flour to baking the bread fed to the chickens, was a waste—and this on top of the excess of the world market price for bread grain over that for chickenfeed.

The inefficiency in Israel's tax system increased significantly at the end of the 1960s, when increased defense expenditure prompted the government to raise the tax rates and to levy new taxes. This is especially noticeable in the income tax. The high marginal tax rates already applied to below-average incomes distorted the whole wage structure. Wage increases were subject to such extremely high marginal tax rates that "incentives" had to be devised to avoid them, and so "indirect arrangements" were developed. A complicated system of disguised compensations grew up, such as covering (fictional) costs of maintaining cars and telephones, or allowances for purchasing books, under the pretense of their being legitimate business expenses. Further "arrangements" took the form of fictitious overtime work or "special efforts," since such compensation was subject to lower income tax rates. Inflation also increased the cost-of-living allowances, which are not subject to income tax. Workers employed on a daily basis often worked only three weeks each month in order to receive sick pay for the fourth week, because the net income from sick pay was higher than the marginal net-after-tax wage for a fourth workweek. Such arrangements—which began as hidden agreements—soon became legitimized and approved—de facto—by the tax authorities. They were formulated in work agreements and their procedures were even set by the tax authorities.[b] Such arrangements have even spread to the employees of the income tax authority itself.

### The Tax System and Income Distribution

One of the main social objectives of the tax system is to reduce the inequality of income. Attaining this objective is accompanied, understandably, by some damage to economic efficiency. An efficient tax system is one that achieves the objective with minimal harm to efficiency. A progressive

[b]For example, according to an agreement made in 1970, each professor in an Israeli university received compensation for car maintenance—"transportation"—even if he did not own a car. The professor had to fill out a monthly form, outlining his routine of "travel" in his automobile. This form was provided by the tax authorities. It was agreed that professors who did not own cars should also submit this form.

income tax, that is, a tax with a higher rate on higher incomes, is an accepted method for reducing inequality. The income tax in Israel is indeed progressive. Its contribution to reducing income inequality is discussed in Chapter 20.

A complaint often heard is that the more progressive the income tax, the greater its damage to economic efficiency, because the high tax rates sharply reduce the net marginal income from work, discourage specialization and weaken the desire to work. On the one hand it reduces incomes, and on the other hand it creates incentives to evade paying taxes. Thus, it is argued that if the tax rates were reduced, economic efficiency would increase, raising both the net income earned by the public and the government's tax receipts.[10]

The harm to efficiency is accepted by society for the sake of the more equal distribution of income. However, Israel's income tax system is distorted to the point where even the contribution to income equalization is lost.

The marginal income tax rates are very high even for incomes below average, while the tax revenue from these incomes is surprisingly low. This is because of the widespread avoidances and evasion. As the rates increase, the incentives for avoiding and evading payment also increase. A statistical analysis of the receipts from income tax over a number of years, conducted by Berglas, shows that an increase in marginal tax rates lowers total taxes collected.[11] This means that marginal rates have reached levels that are so high that their contribution to progressivity is insignificant, while their damage to economic efficiency is severe.

High marginal rates lead to erosion of the income tax base. Such erosion is regressive. For example, cost-of-living allowances that are proportional to income (up to a specific ceiling) are tax-free. Because of the progressive structure of the income tax, the saving in tax is greater at higher income levels. The same holds for the special law limiting the tax rate on overtime to 35 percent. Only those with incomes whose marginal tax is higher than 35 percent can benefit from this concession, and the higher the income the greater is the benefit. Another example is the arrangement for paying salaries disguised as business expenses, and therefore not subject to taxation. These arrangements are made principally for earners with above-average earnings, and the higher the income (with a higher marginal tax rate), the greater will be the benefit enjoyed.

These arrangements, accumulating over the years, resulted in regressive effective tax rates over a certain low range of incomes. In 1972 the loss of certain benefits given only to high incomes raised the effective marginal tax to as much as 80 percent for incomes between IL 400 and IL 600 per month; for those above IL 600 per month marginal taxation fell to 35 percent.

Indirect taxation also aims at reducing inequality of income. The common opinion is that indirect taxes on luxury products are progressive, resulting in a more equal distribution of real income net of tax. For this reason indirect taxes in Israel were levied on a limited number of expensive luxury products and subsidies were granted only to products termed popular.

Taxing a limited number of products at high rates damages economic efficiency. However, to collect high tax revenues, the authorities widened the definition of luxury products and levied indirect taxes on products demanded over a wide income range. It has been found that the share of these products in the family budget decreases as income increases, so that the taxes turned out to be regressive. They increased the inequality of incomes, even though the damage to economic efficiency was accepted as a necessary sacrifice for the sake of decreasing income inequality.

The subsidies, whose purpose is, in part, to reduce inequality of income, are of considerable importance in Israel. However, they are not an efficient instrument for the purpose. These subsidies on products benefit not only low-income earners but high-income earners as well, and the extent of the benefit depends on consumption habits. For instance, consumers with high incomes will benefit more from low meat prices than consumers with low incomes, simply because they eat more meat.

Despite the sharp increase in the commodity prices on the world market as from 1972, the Israeli government kept their prices at home quite fixed, by "pouring" increasing subsidies. The damage to efficiency became increasingly noticeable (it was claimed that sugar and other commodities were smuggled to neighboring Arab countries). In 1973 the government reduced a small part of these subsidies and in 1974, following the 1973 War, finally cut them very sharply. In order to compensate the lower-income groups, direct personal grants were established. In principle this is a better method, since it can reduce the income gap without providing unnecessary subsidies to the wealthy and without damaging economic efficiency. However, these grants were introduced at such a low rate that they failed to compensate effectively the low-income group for the rise in the prices of basic commodities.

**Reform of the Tax System.**   In 1974 Israel was faced by an urgent need for widespread reform in the structure of its tax system. The following are the principal lines that reform should take.

1. Expanding the income-tax base, while relaxing the steepness and lowering the level of the marginal tax rates and abolishing the special arrangements and concessions.—Despite the lowering of the marginal rates, a reformed tax system could raise the same revenue even while maintaining an even higher effective degree of progressivity. This is possible because:

> (a) an expanded tax base will increase revenues; (b) reduced marginal rates will lower avoidance and evasion; (c) increased efficiency of the economy will increase real, taxable income; and (d) the abolition of the special arrangements will increase progressivity.

2. Expanding the base of indirect taxes, with significant reductions in the rates.—Indirect taxes levied on *all* goods and services would raise the same revenues with much lower tax rates. This minimizes the damage to economic efficiency as well as the burden on the taxpayer. In practice, this tax, whether in the form of a turnover tax, on final products, or as a value added tax, is the principal source of revenue in those Western European countries where taxes raise 30 percent or more of the national product. It is not a progressive tax, and to a certain extent it is even regressive. But in comparison to the regressiveness of the current indirect tax system in Israel, it would still be a great improvement for progressivity as well as for economic efficiency.

3. Eliminating all compulsory loans and merging them with the overall tax system.

4. Eliminating subsidies on commodities.

5. Introduction of a "negative income-tax," which is the most effective method of increasing the overall progressivity of the tax system.[c]

In 1970 a public committee was formed in Israel to examine the tax system. The committee's recommendations were all in line with the principles stated above. Special emphasis was put on the recommendation for an introduction of a value added tax, similar to the tax the Common Market countries introduced during the 1960s and early 1970s.[12] Acceptance of the committee's recommendations would correct the distortions in Israel's tax system and place it on a more efficient, more consistent and more just basis.

## NOTES

1. The data here are from the *Bank of Israel Annual Reports,* 1967, 1968, 1971.
2. See *Border Tax Adjustments and Tax Structures in OECD Member Countries* (Paris: OECD, 1968).
3. See *Bank of Israel Annual Report,* 1971.
4. See *Revenue from Taxation in the EEC, 1958–65* (Brussels: Statistical Office, European Community, 1967).
5. E. Berglas, *An Empirical Evaluation of Israel's Income Tax,* 1953–1965, pp. 90–91, in Israel and the Common Market (Ed. P. Uri), Weidenfeld and Nicolson, Jerusalem, 1971.
6. A. Dagan and Maital, "Purchase Tax on Services," *Tax Quarterly,* No. 5, 1967 (in Hebrew).

[c]According to this method, earners with incomes above a certain base level pay taxes on the excess of their incomes over the base income as they do under the existing method. Earners with incomes lower than the base receive a government payment based on the deficiency of their income below the base income. A negative income tax is more effective than the present system in increasing equality of income at the lower end of the scale, where it is most important, because it provides payments to low-income groups, while the present system can, at most, refrain from taxing them.

7. A detailed and extensive discussion, including empirical evaluations, appears in Berglas, op. cit., Chapter 4.

8. Ibid., pp. 123–124.

9. Amoz Morag, *Government Financing in Israel* (Jerusalem: The Magnes Press, 1967), p. 244.

10. Berglas, op. cit.

11. Berglas, op. cit.

12. As early as 1964 Professor A. Morag recommended the introduction of a value added tax in Israel. See "Added Value Tax," *Economic Quarterly*, 41–42, March 1964, pp. 67–73.

# Chapter Eighteen

# Stabilization of the Economy

Economic stabilization and efficiency can prevail only when two conditions exist simultaneously: aggregate demand (total spending by everybody on all goods and services in the economy) must be enough (but not more than enough) to buy at current prices the total possible output under full employment; employers and employees must not raise their prices and wages in efforts to increase or to protect their share in the aggregate output.

## REGULATING AGGREGATE DEMAND

If aggregate demand is greater than full-employment output at current prices, the price of products will rise. This increases profits and causes pressure for wage increases. If this is accompanied by increases in government expenditure and in money supply, aggregate demand keeps on increasing, prices and wages keep on increasing too, and the process continues. This process is called *demand inflation.*

If aggregate demand is less than full-employment output at current prices, production is curtailed, resources are not fully utilized, and there is unemployment.

The government has at its disposal two principal instruments for regulating aggregate demand: *budgetary policy* and *monetary policy.*

Budgetary policy (also called *fiscal policy*) influences aggregate demand in two ways: it determines the volume of government spending; it determines the volume of taxes collected, thereby affecting spending by everybody else. The government can increase aggregate demand by increasing its expenditures or by reducing taxes. These operations may increase a budgetary deficit or decrease a budgetary surplus, or turn a surplus into a deficit. The government can decrease aggregate demand by cutting its expenditures or by increasing taxes.

These operations may increase a budgetary surplus, or reduce a budgetary deficit or turn a deficit into a surplus.

*Monetary policy* influences the level of public spending by regulating the means of payment or money supply—that is, the quantity of money in the hands of the public. A reduction in the quantity of money held by the public normally causes a decline in spending, while an expansion causes an increase in spending. A government usually exerts its quantitative control on money indirectly, through the central bank (in Israel, the Bank of Israel), which operates in close contact with commercial banks.

The quantity of money is regulated in several ways. The most important, in Israel, is the control of banking credit to the public. Extending bank credit automatically increases the quantity of money, while a decline in such credit automatically reduces it. To regulate the volume of credit, banking institutions are required to hold part of their financial assets in specific forms: in deposits with the central bank, in government securities, in cash and in foreign currency. Such required holdings are called "required reserves" because, originally, similar holdings were maintained by banks as reserves against unexpected withdrawals of deposits. In Israel they are called liquid assets. The extent of the required liquid assets is expressed as a required *ratio* to total deposits. This is called the required liquidity ratio. Only the excess of total deposits over the required liquid assets can be used by the banks for loans or credit to their customers. Thus the required liquid assets or required reserves are actually *frozen* assets subject to the control of the central bank, and can serve neither as liquidity nor as available reserves.

In periods of depression, when aggregate demand is low, the central bank can try to increase aggregate demand by reducing the required liquidity ratio. This increases the free reserves of the commercial banks, allowing them to increase credit (loans) to the public, if necessary by lowering the interest rate. This increases the quantity of money in the hands of the public and enables them to increase their expenditures, raising aggregate demand. In periods of inflationary pressure from excessive aggregate demand, the central bank can increase the required liquidity ratio, forcing commercial banks to reduce their loans to the public, thereby decreasing the quantity of money in the hands of the public and lowering aggregate demand.

In a formal sense the central bank is an independent institution. The bank acts as an advisor to the government on matters of economic policy and may influence the government's decisions. In practice, however, the central bank has to adhere to a monetary policy that is consistent with the government's budgetary policy. This coordination is necessary. In a demand inflation, when budgetary policy acts to reduce aggregate demand, monetary policy is normally directed to reducing the money supply; in a period of unemployment, when budgetary policy acts to increase aggregate demand, monetary policy is normally such as to increase the money supply.

As indicated above, in order for stability to persist total aggregate demand must correspond to the total resources available to the economy. These total resources consist of the total domestic output plus imports minus exports. If exports and imports are equal, the total resources available to the economy will exactly equal the value of the domestic output. The current account of the balance of payments, which consists of total payments for imports and total receipts from exports, will then be balanced. The balance of trade is then said to be zero. Where exports are greater than imports, total goods and services available to the economy are less than the total domestic product. The current amount of the balance of payments then shows a surplus. The balance of trade is said to be positive, and we have an *export surplus.* On the other hand, when imports exceed exports, the total of goods and services available to the economy exceed the domestic product. The current account of the balance of payments shows a deficit and the trade balance is negative. This deficit is equal to the *import surplus,* that is, that part of imports not covered by export receipts.

When aggregate demand exceeds the total of domestically available goods and services (so that there is an inflationary pressure), the gap can be closed not only by reducing aggregate demand but also by increasing the supply of goods and services. This can be done either by increasing imports or by decreasing exports. This involves increasing the deficit or decreasing the surplus, or turning a surplus into a deficit, in the balance of payments on current account. In Israel, this has always meant increasing the import surplus (and thus increasing the deficit by the same amount).

An import surplus can last only as long as the economy can keep on paying for it in foreign currency. The reserves of foreign currency can be replenished from several sources: unilateral transfers, foreign loans and foreign investments in the country. When this flow of foreign currency is insufficient to finance the import surplus, the country's foreign currency reserves are diminished. Since these reserves are limited, the import surplus has to be adjusted to the availability of foreign currency sources to pay for it.

Changes in aggregate demand can also affect imports and exports in the opposite direction. When aggregate demand becomes too low, unemployment appears. This reduces the deficit by decreasing imports. It may also increase exports.

### Buyers' and Sellers' Inflation

Inflation caused by excessive aggregate demand may be called buyers' inflation. It is caused by buyers trying to buy more than is available. Inflation can also be caused by *sellers.* Workers selling their labor (for wages) and businessmen selling other productive services and materials may demand more money from the manufacturer than the product can be sold for at current prices. This increase in costs forces the manufacturer to raise the price of the product.

Just as in a buyers' inflation in which the buyers cannot buy more than is available, in a *sellers' inflation* the providers of the productive services cannot earn more than the value of the total product. But as long as these upward pressures on prices and wages continue, we have sellers' inflation[a] with all the undesirable effects.

As inflation continues, maintenance of the existing level of employment and output will call for a continuing increase in money expenditure to buy the same goods and services at higher prices. In the absence of an increase in the money supply or in expansionary fiscal policy, spending will become insufficient and unemployment will grow. There will then be increasing pressure on the government to provide the expansionary monetary and fiscal policy measures to alleviate the depression. Attempts by the authorities to check the inflation by refraining from providing these expansionary measures (which will be denounced as "inflationary" by those who know only about buyers' inflation) will bring about the compromise between full employment and depression, which has been given the label "recession."

If employment is maintained and the inflation (either kind) continues and is not accompanied by a proportional increase in the foreign exchange rate (that is, by devaluation), the competitiveness of exports in foreign markets decreases and the competitiveness of imports in the domestic market increases. This results in a greater trade deficit or import surplus. The increased demand for imported products is a shift in demand *from* domestic products, which also tends to cause unemployment. The decreased demand for exports works in the same direction, too.

As the demand for domestic products declines, unemployment grows in the "recession." If the government wants to prevent or lessen unemployment, it has to increase aggregate demand by budgetary and monetary policies. In this way full employment can be restored, but unsatisfied wage and profit demands will cause prices and wages to rise again, and the process continues. Moreover, even before full employment has been restored, the increase in aggregate demand also raises the demand for imports, thereby further increasing the import surplus. If the country lacks sufficient new sources of foreign currency for financing a continuing and perhaps rising import surplus, its foreign currency reserves will be depleted.

Sellers' inflation would be halted by persuading labor unions and employers' associations to shelve efforts to increase their share of the national cake. If this persuasion fails, the inflation can be reduced by avoiding government action designed to reduce unemployment. As unemployment increases, the demands for increased wages and profits may be weakened and the inflation moderated. Monetary and budgetary policies may thus trade off price stability

[a]The term *cost inflation* is often used in economic literature, but it does not correctly indicate the real cause of the inflation. This kind of inflation is largely derived from the administrative power of labor unions and employers' associations. Accordingly, it is also called *administered inflation*.

against employment (or inflation against unemployment). But it may take a severe and prolonged depression to eliminate the inflationary sellers' pressure on costs and thus on prices.

When full employment and price stability cannot be obtained simultaneously, the government's second-best policy is to maintain an optimal balance between them. The balancing point is where the social damage from a marginal increase in unemployment equals the social benefit from the marginal increase in price stability gained by the increase in unemployment. When this is achieved a certain level of unemployment exists side-by-side with a certain rate of inflation. In general, the social preference should be for a high level of inflation and a low level of unemployment, rather than for a high level of unemployment and a low level of inflation. Therefore, one should expect that at the optimal balancing point employment is almost full, even if the rate of inflation is quite high.

## INSTABILITY IN THE ISRAELI ECONOMY

Between 1950 and 1972 Israel's economy faced fluctuations and instabilities of different types. There were price increases, wage increases, fluctuations in the trade balance, full employment and even a period of unemployment. Thus the processes described above all played a part in the development of Israel's economy.

We now turn to the government's policy on price stability and full employment in the post-1960 period. This may be divided into three subperiods: (1) 1960–1964 were years of full employment, economic growth, increasing inflation and trade deficits (import surpluses); (2) 1965–1967 was a period of recession, unemployment and a reduction in inflation; and (3) 1968–1973 were years of revival, full employment and growth, together with inflation and excessively high trade deficits.

### Government Policy: 1960-1964

In 1960–1964 demand inflation prevailed. Prices rose at 7 percent per annum and the import surplus rose from $300 million in 1959 to $570 million in 1964 (see Chapter 12). Throughout this period the economy was operating at full employment. The growing import surplus reduced the excess aggregate demand and weakened the pressure for price increases. However, the import surplus reached dimensions that threatened to exceed the prospective foreign currency resources. It was thus necessary to take measures to reduce the import surplus. There are two principal ways in which this can be done.

One way is to engage in restrictive monetary and fiscal measures to reduce the income derived from wages and profits. This would decrease aggregate demand and free resources for producing more exports and import substitutes. If the decline in wages and profits results in a price decline, this will increase the competitiveness of the economy in foreign markets, increase exports and reduce imports. But the price reduction must be less than the money-income reduction, so that *real* income is also reduced. The reduction in real income is necessary because resources must be set free to achieve the reduction in the import surplus.

Another way of reducing an import surplus is to raise the exchange rate (that is, devaluation). This brings about an increase in the domestic prices of import products and raises the return on production of exports and import substitutes. It increases the competitiveness of the economy in foreign markets exactly like the price decline discussed above. If wages and profits are not increased and prices of domestic output remain fixed, then, with the increased prices of imports and of exportable goods, real wages and profits will fall. As a result aggregate domestic demand will decline, releasing resources for the production of export products and import substitutes.

These two approaches are fundamentally identical. They both require a decline in real income and aggregate demand along with a drop in domestic prices relative to prices in foreign markets. The first approach would reduce nominal income, relative to prices (while keeping the rate of exchange at a fixed level); the second would raise prices relative to the nominal income (by a devaluation, which raises the exchange rate).

However, the first way is not really available since it is almost impossible to reduce nominal prices. It is less difficult to bring about the necessary decline in real income by raising prices (through devaluation) and keeping nominal income fixed. But governments often reject the second way because of an irrational psychological aversion to devaluation.

**Preventing Price Rises.**   To prevent price rises due to excess aggregate demand, the government could make use of budgetary measures, reducing government expenditures and increasing taxes. As expenditures decrease, aggregate demand falls; as taxes increase, public purchasing power decreases, thus again reducing aggregate demand.

During the years 1960–1964 the government's real expenditures increased more rapidly than the gross national product.[b] Thus government policy, in practice, increased excess aggregate demand instead of reducing it. The government maintained that aggregate demand can be reduced by keeping tax revenues equal to the growing budgetary expenditures, that is, by way of a *balanced budget*. The principle of a balanced budget as a specific measure against excessive aggregate demand and inflationary pressure appeared in almost every speech by the Finance Minister on the state of the budget.[1]

But a balanced budget does not prevent inflation, or even contribute to reducing inflation. It might seem that a balanced budget is neutral with respect

[b]The real expenditures include government consumption in its current account (the "regular budget") and government investment in its capital account (the "development budget"). These expenditures do not include payments abroad for redemption of foreign loans, which do not affect domestic aggregate demand.

to aggregate demand, but it is not neutral; it actually contributes to aggregate demand. The balanced budget does indeed require taxing the public, and this taxation reduces income and expenditures, but these taxes are used to finance government acquisition of goods and services from the public. The taxed income thus returns to the public as income earned in supplying goods to the government. Public net income remains at its original level and therefore expenditure by the public is not reduced. On top of this there is the expenditure by the government. A balanced budget thus contributes to aggregate demand by an amount exactly equal to the government expenditure, that is, by the total of the budget. An increasing balanced budget is of course increasingly inflationary.

Moreover, what was known in Israel as a "balanced budget" was not balanced at all, since not all government expenditures are financed by taxes. The "balanced budget" accepted by the government included only current budget expenditures. But government expenditure on capital account—that is, providing loans and making investments—which is not included, has exactly the same influence on aggregate demand.

A genuinely neutral budget, with respect to aggregate demand, would have to raise in taxes an amount that covered not only expenditures on capital account as well as on current account (that is, *all* government expenditures), but raise, in addition to this, further taxes (that is, to show a surplus in the budget) sufficient to reduce incomes by such an amount that the public would cut *their* spending by the total amount spent by the government. Even that would not contribute to *reducing* the (inflationary) excess demand, but would merely make the budget neutral. It would only prevent it from aggravating the inflation. The principles of budgetary policy for reducing inflationary pressure must, therefore, be formulated in another way.

To reduce aggregate demand, government expenditures must either be lowered or taxes increased, or both together. If there is a deficit in the government's budget to begin with, this deficit will be reduced by these measures, and perhaps converted into a surplus. If there is already a surplus in the government's budget, these measures will make the surplus bigger. The government should consciously use its budget, with surpluses or deficits, to influence aggregate demand. The principle of balancing the budget has no relevance to a policy designed to stabilize the economy.

It is a commonly held opinion that taxes are required in order to finance government expenditure. This opinion is erroneous. *Taxes are not required for financing government expenditure.* These expenditures can be easily financed out of deficits; and when aggregate demand is too low, this is the proper way. This means that the government does not have a problem in financing its expenditures. The principal function of taxes is to *assist in regulating the level of the aggregate demand.* Thus, taxes must be included within the framework of "functional finance."

In the years 1963–1964 it seemed that the government had succeeded in producing a budgetary surplus, since in the current account income from taxes was greater than expenditures (by IL 103 million in 1963 and by IL 262 million in 1964). However, if government investments are taken into account, it is found that the government caused a net increase in aggregate demand. This increase was especially high in 1962 and 1964 and relatively lower in 1963.[2]

Thus, while appearing to reduce inflationary pressure, the government really was increasing it. This increased aggregate demand was partly absorbed by increased import surpluses. There still remained excess demand, however, which caused prices to rise.

The increase in the money supply, which took place during the same period, also played its part in the increase in aggregate demand. The money supply increased in 1962 by 30 percent and in 1963 by 28 percent. Only in 1964 did the rate of increase lessen, to 6 percent. The Bank of Israel did increase the banks' required reserve ratio, but a large inflow of foreign currency, converted to local currency, provided the public with an additional money supply. A government surplus budget could have absorbed at least part of the additional money supply. However, in view of the deficits in the government budgets, the Bank of Israel was unable to prevent the expansion of the money supply.

**Decreasing the Import Surplus.**   Decreasing the trade deficit requires not only a reduction of aggregate demand, but, as we have seen, also a decrease in prices, profits, and wages relative to foreign countries. As has been said, this can be achieved either by an overall decrease in prices and wages, or by an increase in the rate of exchange (a devaluation of the country's currency).

Quite frequently the Israeli government was advised to take measures designed to *decrease* wages and prices. The government, however, limited itself to the more modest goal of *preventing increases* in wages and prices. Yet even this modest goal was not achieved, and a trend of continuous rises in wages and prices prevailed. This trend resulted from the pressure of excess aggregate demand, which created demand inflation. As we saw in Chapter 16, as long as demand inflation persists it is impossible for administrative measures to prevent increases in wages and prices.

The increase in wages and prices created pressure on the government to take the other route for reducing the import surplus, that is, to devalue the currency. Israel's economy has followed a process of continuous hidden devaluation, in the form of tariff increases on imports and increasing subsidies for exports. Every few years a devaluation would be made which, in practice, constituted official recognition of the effective exchange rate that was already in force. This rate was also applied to capital transfers. The method of gradual "hidden devaluations," however, accompanied by sporadic official devaluations, did not achieve its purpose. The import surplus was not reduced, but increased yearly, from $300 million in 1959 to a peak of $570 million in 1964.

The reason for this failure lies in the fact that prices and wages increased, and so the gradual devaluation did not change the level of prices and wages relative to foreign countries. Moreover, if the import surplus had not increased, prices and wages would have risen even faster. Thus these increases in import surplus and wages and prices all resulted from the excess aggregate demand, which was not reduced by the government but rather increased. The reason for the government's failure to stabilize the level of prices and wages is the same as the reason for its failure to reduce the deficit in the current amount of the balance of payments.

Many factors prevented the government from reducing the excess demand in the period prior to 1965. One factor was immigration. The absorption of the immigrants had a direct effect on the budget and on aggregate demand. The main items of expenditure related to immigration are: building of dwellings; providing education, health services and welfare; and making investments to provide for their employment. To meet these obligations without creating excess demand the government would have had to cut back on other expenditures and to increase taxes. But here the government encountered—and yielded to—strong public opposition.

As long as immigration continued the government could not reduce aggregate demand, although this was an objective officially stated in the economic policy principles formulated in 1962. Only after immigration declined from 60,000 a year during 1962-1964 to 30,000 in 1965 and then to 15,000 in 1966 and 1967 did the government succeed in reducing the rate of increase of its expenditures. Thus the government was able to reduce its contribution to increasing aggregate demand not on its own initiative but because of an external factor, namely, the reduction in immigration.

### Government Policy: 1965-1967

In 1965 there was a significant increase in the wage level. This was a delayed reaction to the excess demand and inflation of 1963-1964, when wage increases were held in check over a long period of negotiation on wage agreements. When the wage increases were granted, the government's policy of reducing investments and expenditures was already underway. This had a depressing influence on the economy. The rate of increase in the money supply also declined to 11 percent in 1965 and to 6 percent in 1966. The decline in aggregate demand brought about severe unemployment, which began in the building industry and then spread to other sectors. In spite of the declining aggregate demand and unemployment, prices continued to rise at a rate similar to that of the years 1962-1964, namely 7-8 percent per annum. The economy moved from demand inflation into sellers' inflation, accompanied by unemployment. Only in 1967, when unemployment had reached a rate of over 10 percent of the labor force, did price and wage rises come to a halt. The deficit in the current account of the balance of payments—the import surplus—fell from IL 570 million in 1964 to IL 450 million in 1966.

The price paid for these achievements was too high. In this situation there were two options open to the government. One option was to increase aggregate demand by increasing government expenditures. But this option would have brought back rising prices, increasing wages and a growing import surplus. The second option was a substantial improvement in the profitability of exports and import substitutes, achieved by raiding the effective exchange rate—either by devaluation or by a system of import tariffs and export subsidies—thereby reducing the import surplus. The increased employment resulting from this policy also would have restored pressure for price and wage increases; but by then the import surplus would have been reduced and the benefits would have outweighed the harm.

At the beginning of 1967 it seemed as though the government were taking appropriate steps to encourage exports by expanding its so-called "incentives." An opportunity had apparently arrived for the government to bring about the change in the structure of the economy required to lower the import surplus while retaining full employment, thus reducing the economic dependence of the country. However, as we have seen (Chapter 13), the "incentives" generated different effective exchange rates and did not follow the principles of economic efficiency. The incentives were, in fact, insufficient as well as inefficient, and the resulting (multiple) effective exchange rate for exports remained too low to channel the unemployed factors into exports.

Government opposition to a substantial increase in the exchange rate and the sociopolitical pressure resulting from unemployment forced the government to take emergency measures to increase domestic aggregate demand and employment through public works and investment in the infrastructure. These started at the beginning of 1967. With increased defense expenditures, following the Six-Day War, the process gained momentum. As a result, the economy headed toward a renewed demand inflation, accompanied by rising wages and prices and growing import surpluses. The opportunity to move the economic structure in the desired direction was missed.

Government policy during the recession led to only a temporary reduction in the import surplus, and that at great social cost in terms of unemployment, reduction of output and the curbing of economic growth. "The cost of the dollar which was saved in this way, reached, in the final analysis, IL 9."[3]

### Government Policy: 1968–1973
The period 1968–1973 saw an unprecedented increase in government spending. The seriousness of the security situation following the Six-Day War in 1967 and the War of Attrition of 1969–1970 led to a rapid increase in defense expenditures. While in 1966 these expenditures constituted some 9 percent of the GNP, in 1970 they reached a peak of 25 percent. In 1972 they were down to 21 percent. With the war of 1973 they increased to 35 percent. With the revival of immigration there was also a significant increase in expenditures to meet the

immigrants' needs. This was reflected especially in increasing government investment in housing. Rising social tensions resulted in increased expenditure on
social services, and the problems of the cities required the investment of large
sums in the development of urban infrastructures. As a result, by 1972 public
consumption (in real terms) was three times that of 1967.

With the rise in government spending there was also a substantial
increase in tax rates. Taxes, as a percentage of the national product, rose from
26.5 percent in 1967 to 37.3 percent in 1972. If we include the compulsory
loans, taxes reached 41.1 percent in 1972. But even that was not sufficient to
cover the increase in government spending. The budget deficit—the excess of
government spending over taxes collected—rose from IL 2 billion in 1967 to
approximately IL 4 billion in 1972.

These developments put an end to the recession, and in 1969 the
economy reached full employment. Moreover, the increasing economic activity
actually resulted in excess demand for labor, which was partly supplied by the
rapid increase of Arab employment coming in from the West Bank and the Gaza
Strip. In 1973 Arab labor employed in Israel grew to more than 5 percent of
the labor force of the country.

This economic resurgence included significant increases in investment
and private consumption. Investment (at fixed prices) rose in 1968 by 48 percent, and in 1973 it was more than three times that of 1967. Private consumption
increased rapidly in 1968 and 1969 (8 percent per capita per annum). The rate
of increase then slowed to 1 percent per capita per annum, but in 1972 and 1973
again increased to 6 percent per capita per annum. The total increase in real
consumption between 1967 and 1972 was 30 percent per capita and almost 60
percent for the economy.

The rapid increase in government expenditures, investments and
private consumption surpassed the rate of increase of the national product, despite the fact that the national product itself (in fixed prices) was, in 1973,
almost 75 percent higher than in 1967.

The gap between total aggregate expenditures and the domestic
product thus increased. It was directly reflected in a rapid increase in imports
far surpassing the increase in exports, that is, in a rapid increase in the import
surplus, from $530 million in 1967 to $1.3 billion in 1970 and $2.5 billion in
1973 (of which about $1 billion was a direct effect of the 1973 War).

The money supply rose from IL 2 billion at the end of 1967 to
IL 5.6 billion by 1972 and to IL 7.4 billion by the end of 1973, with the highest
rates of increase after 1971. The principal factor in the increase in this money
supply was government borrowing from the commercial banks and from the
Bank of Israel to finance its budget deficit, especially during 1968–1970 when
a decline in foreign currency reserves cancelled part of the effect on the money
supply. During 1971 and 1973, however, the flow of foreign currency into the
country increased the foreign exchange reserves from $400 million to $1.8 bil-

lion. This accelerated the increase of the money supply, which rose during these years at close to 30 percent per annum.

Coming together, the increased economic activity, the rise in the aggregate expenditures at a rate greater than that of the national product and the rapid increase in the means of payment exerted considerable inflationary pressure. In 1970 the price level resumed its increase at a rate of 12–14 percent per annum, and in 1973 prices rose by 28 percent. This rise in prices was accompanied by a corresponding wage rise, in a self-reinforcing inflationary cycle.

In 1968 and 1969 government policy was especially notable for its passivity. In spite of the dynamic changes the economy was undergoing the government took no comprehensive action to influence it. Its only measure was an increase in taxes. During this period the economy was in transition from recession to inflation, undergoing a short period of stability. Thus in 1968 and 1969 prices and wages were stable and unemployment was fading away.

The government's lack of action cannot easily be explained by supposing that everything seemed to be going well. The balance-of-payments deficit was growing very rapidly, and by 1969 foreign currency holdings were falling at a dangerous rate. Despite these alarming signals the government took no action.

The beginning of 1970 brought hopes of a turning point in government policy. Plans were drawn up for levying additional taxes and for devaluating the currency. The program was designed to absorb consumer purchasing power (and thus reduce the rate of increase in aggregate demand), and to channel economic resources primarily into export production (by improving the exchange rate for exporters), while raising the prices of imported products.

However, political pressures prevented the government from implementing its program. Pressure from the labor unions for higher wages and pressure from the manufacturers to increase prices led the government to abandon the program in favor of a three-sided compromise agreement (the "package deal"). According to the terms of this agreement the workers were to give up part of their claims for wage increases, the manufacturers were to cease pressing for price increases and the government was to drop most of its plans for raising taxes.

The "package deal" was, in fact, a continuation of the government policy of inaction. However, the events of 1970 and 1971 show that the government did not honor its part of the package deal. In April 1970, direct taxes were raised to a rate higher than was implied in the agreement, and national insurance rates were raised substantially, too. In August 1970, premiums of 20 percent were granted to most of the exports, a 20 percent across-the-board tariff on imports was imposed and additional indirect taxes were levied. These steps, although in conflict with the package deal, were in the right direction, since they absorbed purchasing power from the public, encouraged exports and discouraged imports. An additional step in the right direction was taken in August 1971 with the devaluation of the currency from IL 3.50 to IL 4.20 per dollar.

As a result there was a significant decline in the rate of increase in private consumption (in 1970 real consumption per capita increased by only 1 percent) and in the import surplus. In 1971 and 1972 the import surplus even declined a little (though this was attributed to some technical delays in transferring military equipment). In sum, the steps actually taken by the government in 1970 and 1971 were in the right direction but on too small a scale.

In 1972, for the first time since 1967, the government tried to reduce the real level of government spending for public consumption. With increased immigration and strong social pressures for increased public services, an attempt was made to reduce defense expenditures. This was finally done on a very small scale. But at the same time taxes stopped increasing, and even decreased somewhat. There was, thus, no diminution in the inflationary pressures: A rise in private consumption more than offset the minor decline in public spending; and the inflationary price-increase was accelerated. The severity of the situation was obscured by the huge flow of foreign currency in 1972, which increased the foreign exchange reserves. As was stated, this increased the money supply, further facilitating inflationary pressure.

In 1973, while the economy was already under considerable demand inflation pressures, the government took actions that increased these pressures. It reduced taxes and increased subsidies on the export of commodities (to hold down their prices, which had risen sharply on the international market), thus increasing its budgetary deficit. This resulted in a sharp rise in private consumption (close to 10 percent per capita) and in imports, increasing the import surplus by 40 percent. Prices in 1973 were increasing at an annual rate of 25 percent.

Thus, in the summer of 1973, the Israeli economy was undergoing sharp inflation, a jump in the balance-of-payments deficit and a rapid increase in the standard of living. All these were accompanied by enormous pressures for wage increases and intensifying social struggles. Government policy was again inactive, just as in 1969.[c]

### Economic Policy after the 1973 War

Israel was facing a severe inflation and an increasing trade deficit when the 1973 War broke out. The war increased the magnitude of these two problems much further. In order to reduce the rate of inflation and bring down the trade deficit, the government took a number of drastic fiscal steps. It increased the income tax rates, imposed a compulsory loan, increased the tariff rates on imports, cut down the subsidies to essential commodities, reduced its

[c]The fact that the government did not cause an effective recession before 1965, did not take antiinflationary actions in 1969 but rather in 1970, and abandoned its restraining policy in 1973, is probably explained by the general elections that took place in those years. In general, there is quite significant evidence that cycles in government policy may be correlated with the timing of election.

expenditures on nondefense items and administratively checked building activities, especially for public services. The Bank of Israel took steps to eliminate the increase in the money supply.

These steps were all in the right direction, but their effectiveness was far from complete. Total defense expenditures increased tremendously. This caused a big budgetary deficit and pushed up the money supply, despite the Bank of Israel's tight-money policy. The increase in income tax rates aggravated the inefficiency of the economic system.

The government did not devalue the Israeli pound, depriving itself of a most effective tool to control the deficit in the balance of payments. The government also reduced the rate of interest on its newly issued bonds, crippling its demand absorption capacity.

Thus, at the end of 1974, further and more effective economic policy steps had to be made by the government in order to stabilize the economy. control the deficit in the balance of payments and improve the efficiency of the tax system.

## NOTES

1. "Our program for next year is thus based on the following principles: (1) a balanced government budget." "The Budget Law of 1963–1964, 31/12/62," *Knesset Minutes,* vol. 35/10, p. 641.

    "I will now review the Principles of our Policy for Next Year. These principles are: balancing the government budget." "The Budget Law of 1964–1965, 23/12/65," *Knesset Minutes,* vol. 38/10, p. 559.

    "The budget we are presenting for the Knesset's endorsement is balanced and adjusted to the government's general policy. The budget is prepared, first and foremost, to continue preserving stability." Ibid.

    Incidentally, this policy was identical with the government's views during the demand inflation of the early 1950s. For example, "One of the most important conditions in curbing the inflation is a balanced budget." *Knesset Minutes,* vol. 7/9, December 20, 1950, p. 539.

2. For a detailed description, see M. Heth, *The Flow of Funds in the Israeli Economy, 1959–1966* (Jerusalem: Bank of Israel, 1968), Chapter X, pp. 217–256.

3. M. Beham and A. Kleiman, "The Cost of Recession," *Banking Quarterly,* June 1968.

# Chapter Nineteen

# Public Services

With the increase of real income per capita resulting from the growth process there is a relatively rapid rate of increase in the demand for public services. These services can be divided into several groups: social services (such as education, health, welfare activities); physical infrastructural services (physical planning, transportation planning, development of transportation systems, supply of water, electricity, communication, such as telephone service and so on); and services designed to preserve the natural environment (liquid and nonliquid garbage incineration, prevention of air and water pollution, flood prevention, provision for green areas, open space and landscape), and preservation of the social and political environment (provision of law, police, defense, and so forth).

These public services (and we have listed only the major ones) are primarily produced, supplied and allocated by administrative organizations—especially central and local governments, with the market mechanism playing a very small, even negligible, role.

The reason is that these are either social goods (such as defense services), or services with significant externalities (such as preservation of the natural environment, physical planning), or services with economies on a scale that is bound to make them natural monopolies (such as the water system, sewerage, electricity). Among them are also services that represent social preferences (such as education and health) and services that are designed to increase the equality of income division (welfare and aid to low-income families, aid to old people, to the retarded, and so on). Many of these public services represent, in fact, a combination of some of these characteristics.

The higher the level of development of the economy the bigger is the proportion of resources allocated to the production and supply of public services. For this reason, as the economy grows, the share of the resources not administered by the market mechanism and the price system increases. Such a development has been taking place in Israel.

The increase in the importance of public services calls for greater attention to the question of the economic efficiency of their allocation and division. In principle there are three main possible ways of administering the system: (1) central administration; (2) decentralization via the market; and (3) decentralized administration.

The production and allocation of public services by central administration has great disadvantages of the type that have been enumerated in the first part of this book. However, use of the market mechanism also suffers from very significant disadvantages since, as we have seen, the pure market does not deal efficiently with social goods, that is, with products involving externalities and social preferences.

The third possibility, decentralized administration, requires that the production and allocation of public services be delegated by the central organization to organizations or bodies that specialize in limited aspects of the system. Despite the advantages of such a decentralized system, it also suffers from numerous deficiencies.

First, there exists a constraint on the total resources available for the whole system. The allocation of the scarce resources must therefore take into account the alternative use of these resources in relation to other services and in other regions. This requires an overall review and a simultaneous decision. Decentralized organizations, however, which have authority over only a partial area, are unable to take such an overall view. Second, there are interrelations among the various services both in the production and in the utility they provide. Efficient allocation must take these interrelations into consideration while decentralized administration cannot. Finally, preferences for different public services vary from one social group to another. Decentralized administration cannot take into consideration these various preferences and act accordingly.

Decentralization via the market is flexible, reacting to changes in alternative costs and preferences by the adjustment of market prices assuring thereby an efficient allocation of scarce resources. Decentralized administration, which is based on bureaucratic organization, is inevitably afflicted by stiffness and inflexibility. In such a system it is natural that local interests and considerations, not in line with efficiency requirements, affect the decisions. This is bound to result in inefficient allocation of resources among different services, among geographical regions and among social groups. One of the indicators of such inefficiency is the lack of consistency in reaching decisions on the same question. For example, there are cases in which one department gives a high preference to a certain service and allocates resources to it despite the fact that it involves high marginal cost, while at the same time another department, in which the marginal cost of the same service is very low, reduces its supply. If a market mechanism of trading among departments had existed, it would, of course, have been able to improve the efficiency of the public services systems.

It is clear, therefore, that an efficient system for the production and allocation of public services requires an appropriate combination of the three methods mentioned above: central administration, decentralized administrations and market mechanism; each of these methods being applied within the range where it is relatively more efficient.

Despite this conclusion, one finds that the process of production and allocation of public services in developed countries is done primarily by decentralized administration of two types: *geographical* (such as regional governments and municipalities) and *functional* (such as offices of the central government for specific tasks or functions). A functional division is also found within regional governments, municipalities and other local authorities. Direct relations and inter-relations exist among all these types of organizations. Each of them administers the allocation of resources for which it is responsible, making use of managerial techniques and tools, the most important of which is the budget. Preparation of the budget means making decisions regarding the allocation of resources in order to supply the different services and to allocate them to different beneficiaries.

### The Public Service System in Israel

The increase in the public service system in Israel has been rapid. The complexity of the tasks and the need for rapidly increasing administrative capacity contributed greatly to the inefficiency of the system. The symptoms of inefficiency appear in two spheres. One is in the managerial process, which includes planning, decisionmaking, operation and control; the second is in policymaking. In the managerial process one can find a variety of weaknesses.

First, there is no real connection between long-range planning and current decisions. For example, decisions by municipalities and local authorities regarding allocation of land for building activities are not coordinated with long-term master plans of the same authorities.

Second, the bureaucratic system encourages the development of routine and inefficient procedures in resource allocation. For example, the budget allocated for a specific activity by a particular department in a given year is rigidly tied to that of the preceding year.

Third, the ability to attract resources and benefits for different services at different localities depends, to a great extent, on informal personal relations and only to a smaller degree on formal, impersonal and relevant criteria. For example, the mayor of a city can mobilize a greater budget for a certain service if he has good relations with the heads of the central government ministry in charge of that service.

Fourth, there is an excessive tendency for the use of administrative tools just because they are easy to handle, even if their contribution to efficiency is negative. For example, an excessive use of earmarked budgets (that is, activities which pay for themselves) introduces stiffness, inflexibility and, of course, inefficiency.

Fifth, there is a lack of correspondence in the level of professional officers, in the various ministries and organizations, who have to cooperate with one another. For example, regional planning committees, which have to approve the development plans of cities in their region, consist of officers at relatively low levels despite the fact that their formal authority supersedes that of the city mayors.

Sixth, managerial control becomes an end in itself, instead of a tool for increasing efficiency. For example, once the annual budget of an administrative authority is determined and the allocation to each service is made and approved, the head of the authority cannot make even small marginal changes even when he finds that certain expenditures are not needed at all, while others, much more essential, are not available because of lack of funds.

In making policy for the allocation of resources several harmful approaches—which may damage efficiency—are in use. The central government often undertakes to match funds to the local authorities for certain activities. As a result, the marginal cost to the local authority of this particular activity becomes lower than its real marginal cost to the economy. This encourages excessive concentration on that activity and results in waste. In addition it also encourages an undesirable and unfavorable division of income, since the richer local governments can raise more funds and thereby receive a greater share of central government support.

There are some services that are provided free, on the margin, thereby encouraging excessive use and waste. An example of this is the public health system, where the charge is in the form of a lump sum, irrespective of the amount of services used. As a result the level of visits to doctors and the level of consumption of medicinal drugs in Israel is one of the highest in the world, implying at least some waste.

### Improving Efficiency

In view of the inefficiency of the public services system, and in light of its increasing importance, there is an increasing need to reform the system. Otherwise the growth of the system will cause inordinate damage to efficiency. The main principles of such reform are as follows:

**Improving the Allocation Mechanism.** The mechanism of allocating central government resources to the decentralized organizations can be reformed to increase efficiency. For example, introducing a system of nonspecific government grants to municipal authorities can improve efficiency in this sphere. These grants would be designed on such a scale that would make it possible for the local authority to provide local services at a minimum level as determined by social norms. At the same time each municipal authority would be free to increase the standards of certain services, on its own account, carrying thereby the full marginal cost. This would lead to efficient allocation of its funds. Such a mechanism could also help to improve income distribution, since localities with lower income might receive larger grants from the central government, enabling them to reach the normal level of services.

**Greater Use of Market and Price Mechanism.** Despite the limitations on the applicability of the market mechanism for the provision of public goods, there are some specific areas in which it is more efficient than centralized administration, and yet there has not been sufficient use of the market. For example, some of the natural monopolies can be organized as public utilities, i.e., as publicly owned commercial firms, differing from monopolistic behavior in their setting of prices. Such organizations can apply, for example, to electricity, water, post and communication. It can also apply to certain transportation services, such as toll roads, and to some health services.

**Improving the Efficiency of Decentralized Administrative Units.** Setting efficient managerial methods for big organizations, in which a great deal of activity is conducted without the help of the market mechanism, is difficult and complex. Many attempts have been made to develop such methods, but achievements to date are not very great. However, on the basis of economic theory and with the help of organizational techniques that have been developed during recent years, some successful experiments have been made, and there is room for more. We refer, primarily, to what is popularly called cost-benefit analysis. Such improvements must, of course, be based on principles of efficiency. It requires the development of an accurate definition of the service programs and the resulting benefits and costs. The data relevant for such analyses should be correctly defined, collected, organized, and processed.

The utilization and application of such efficient methods cannot succeed, however, unless they are properly integrated with the social, political and cultural environment of the administrative organization. Therefore, it is not enough to develop new techniques and to make them operational. It is, rather, essential to find ways and means to increase the intellectual and professional level of all participants in the system of public services and to increase their interest in utilizing such methods. The lessons and experience that have been acquired, for example, in the United States' public system (such as the PPBS— Planning, Programming, Budgeting System) can be learned, adjusted and properly applied in many developing countries.

The process of improvement in efficiency is very difficult and slow. However, its importance is so great that it deserves special attention and major effort.

# Chapter Twenty

# Income Distribution

Income distribution is an issue of major importance, both economically and socially. It has aroused political and social conflicts and has influenced social and economic development in many countries. First and foremost, income distribution is a social problem; nevertheless, it has significant economic implications. This chapter will examine Israel's government policy with regard to this problem.

We have seen that economic efficiency of production is achieved through the market mechanism, when the price of each production factor is equal to the value of its marginal product. This also determines income distribution. Wage levels and wage differentials are determined by the value of the marginal product. The owners of capital and land also earn income according to the value of the marginal product of their property. The division of ownership of land and capital, and the relative skillfulness and productivity of the different workers, determine the distribution of income and the degree of inequality.

If capital and land were divided equally among the population, and if there were no differences in the productivity of labor, there would be very little income inequality. But these conditions do not exist, and income distribution often reaches a degree of inequality unacceptable by society. The government is able to increase the equality of income by using different tools. These include (1) direct taxation, that is, taxation of income; (2) indirect taxation, specifically, taxation (and subsidization) of selected goods and services; (3) provision of social services to different social groups; and (4) manipulation of production factor prices.

The use of such tools may impair economic efficiency. The government's concern should be to improve the income distribution up to the desired level with minimal damage to economic efficiency. It can achieve this goal if it selects the proper tools. In our discussions of the principles of efficient economic policy we pointed out that these tools are taxes properly imposed and subsidies properly granted. Furthermore, in trying to reduce inequality it is worthwhile to utilize means that can achieve other specific goals at the same time. For example, providing health services can be combined with improving income distribution by subsidizing health services to low-income earners. It is also possible to utilize measures that will increase economic efficiency. Limiting the strength of monopolies will usually improve both the distribution of income and economic efficiency. The same holds for encouraging activities with external benefits, such as education. These, too, can serve to increase income equality.

It is possible, however, that in spite of all these efforts the degree of equalization of income will not be sufficient. Then other actions must be taken, even if they cause a certain damage to efficiency. The government would then have to weigh the damage to economic efficiency caused by the marginal change in income distribution against the marginal social value achieved by virtue of the improvement. As long as the damage to efficiency is the minimum possible, the action may be considered efficient.

### Income Inequality in Israel

The degree of income inequality in Israel has been one of the lowest in the world. Information provided by the tax offices of different countries shows—in terms of the Lorenz index of inequality[a]—that in the 1950s Denmark, Britain, Sweden, the United States and Holland had greater income inequality than did Israel.[1] According to information made available from other sources, Israel, Denmark and Holland were among the countries with the lowest level of inequality; the United States, Britain and Japan were among the countries occupying the middle ground of income inequality;[2] among the countries with the highest inequality were Italy, Puerto Rico and Ceylon. A similar conclusion was reached by G. Hanoch.[3]

Over the years the inequality of income in Israel increased. The Lorenz index shows a rise from 0.293 in 1954 to 0.369 in 1964. This rise continued until 1967, but from then on there was something of a decline. In 1969 the Lorenz Index level went up again to 0.372. Nevertheless, the pattern of income distribution in 1969 differed quite significantly from that of 1964, as shown by Table 20-1.

Table 20-1 shows the income distribution for each fifth of the population, as defined by income levels. In 1954 the lowest fifth received 7 percent of the total income; in 1964, 5.1 percent; and in 1969, 5.8 percent. The highest fifth received 38 percent of the total income in 1954; 42.9 percent in 1964; and 44 percent in 1969. An increase in equality implies a transfer of income from families with income higher than the average to families with income lower than

---

[a]This index shows the degree of divergence from absolute equality in the distribution of income, ranging from 0 when income is equally distributed, to 1 when all income is concentrated in the hands of a single family, or a single individual.

**Table 20-1. Gross Income Distribution in Israel, 1954-1964**

| *Income Groups* | *Percentage of Total Income* | | |
|---|---|---|---|
| *(quintiles)* | *1954* | *1964* | *1969* |
| Lowest | 7.0 | 5.1 | 5.8 |
| Second | 13.9 | 11.5 | 10.9 |
| Third | 18.2 | 16.9 | 16.1 |
| Fourth | 22.9 | 23.6 | 23.2 |
| Fifth | 38.0 | 42.9 | 44.0 |
| Total | 100.0 | 100.0 | 100.0 |

Sources: 1954-1964: *Report of the Committee for Inquiring into the Distribution of National Income in Israel,* 1966; 1969: *Report of the Committee for Inquiring into the Development of Incomes and the Social Gap,* 1971.

the average. The increased inequality is reflected in the fact that the income that would need to be transferred in order to achieve full equality increased from 20.4 percent of total income in 1954 to 26.5 percent in 1964, and 27.2 percent in 1969. This measure is called the Index of Differentials.[4]

The government can and does reduce the inequality of income by using several tools. The first of these is the progressive income tax. And indeed, the deduction of the income tax from gross income reduces the Lorenz index of inequality of distribution from 0.293 to 0.265 in 1954; from 0.369 to 0.324 in 1964 and from 0.372 to 0.334 in 1969.[5] The Index of Differentials is also reduced by the income tax: in 1954 from 20.9 percent before tax to 18.6 percent after tax; in 1964 from 26.5 percent to 23.1 percent; and in 1969 from 27.2 percent to 23.9 percent.

A second tool that influences the inequality of income is the use of indirect taxes and subsidies. It was found (see Chapter 17) that indirect taxes in fact *increased* inequality (they were thus regressive) and subsidies, while acting to reduce inequality, only partially offset the effect of the indirect taxes.

The third tool that has a significant effect on income inequality is the provision of social services. These services were found to lessen income inequality.

A measurement of the overall effect of government policy on inequality of incomes was made in Israel for only one year, 1960. It was found that the net effect of all taxes on the reduction of inequality was quite small because the progressive effect of the income tax was largely offset by the regressive effect of indirect taxes. The Lorenz Index showed a decline from 0.314 for income before taxes to 0.300 for income net of all taxes. However, government social services made a significant contribution to reducing the inequality, decreasing the Lorenz Index to 0.234 for income including government services.[b]

[b]These findings, however, are based on partial investigations only.

The fourth tool that affects the distribution of income is the manipulation of production-factor prices. Such prices have been manipulated by the government to obtain various objectives of its economic policy. One of these objectives, though in practice not of highest priority, was the reduction of income inequality. Maintaining low wage differentials is one example of this policy. Charging low prices for leased agricultural land and for water used in agriculture was apparently aimed at insuring a higher income level to agricultural settlers. Setting low interest rates was also designed to increase equality of income, on the assumption that the rich usually lend to the poor. This, however, has not been the case in Israel, where the government lends money to many groups in society, with the rich having a share in these loans greater than their proportion in the society. With the high rate of inflation in the 1970s, these low interest rates became negative in real terms. Thus interest-rate policy in Israel had an adverse effect on the distribution of income.

### Conclusion

The effect of government activities on the distribution of income can be summarized as follows: the progressive income tax increases equality; indirect taxes and subsidies reduce it; social services again increase it; and factor-price manipulation has an ambiguous effect. Despite these inconsistent influences, we can confidently conclude that the net result in Israel was an increase in income equality.

Whatever the improvement in income equality has been, however, it was achieved by inefficient methods. This is substantiated by the following considerations. First, the progressiveness of the income tax system has been inefficiently constructed. We have already discussed this in detail in chapter 17, where we also indicated how income tax efficiency can be increased while retaining its contribution to increased income equality. Second, indirect taxes were also shown to be inefficient. Here the problem is even more severe because these taxes are regressive, thus adversely affecting income distribution. Third, the use of social services is also inefficient in many respects, as we saw in Chapter 19, with reference to health services and the like. Fourth, the manipulation of production-factor prices is a particularly inefficient method as explained at length in several preceding chapters, not to mention the ambiguity of its net effect on distribution of income.

It seems to us that the Israeli government could attain the same net distribution of income and benefits as it actually achieved, or even a greater equality of income distribution, with less waste and inefficiency, by giving up factor-price manipulation and by adopting the reforms proposed for the income tax structure, the system of indirect taxation and subsidies, and in the policy regarding public—and particularly social—services.

## NOTES

1. *Report of the Committee for Inquiring into the Distribution of National Income in Israel,* 1966, p. 65.
2. I.B. Kravis, "International Differences in the Distribution of Income," *Review of Economics and Statistics* 42 (November 1960): 408–417.
3. G. Hanoch, *Income Differentiation in Israel* (Jerusalem: Falk Institute of Economic Research, 1961), pp. 103–129.
4. See N. Zandberg, "Income Distribution, Savings and Consumption," *Economic Quarterly,* No. 15, March 1957.
5. See *Report of the Committee for Inquiring into the Distribution of Income in Israel,* op. cit., p. 217; and *Report of the Committee for Inquiring into the Development of Incomes and the Social Gap,* 1971, p. 27.

# Chapter Twenty-one

# Government Enterprises

The Israeli government is directly involved in many kinds of economic and business activities, carried out by three types of organization: government corporations, government departments and statutory authorities. Government corporations are corporations in which the government owns not less than 25% of the equity capital. There are more than 100 of these in Israel. Government departments are ministerial departments that provide different kinds of public services, such as postal services and telephones (in the Ministry of Communications) and railways (in the Ministry of Transportation). Statutory authorities are bodies that operate under special laws, such as the Bank of Israel, the Port Authority, and several production and marketing boards. These bodies produce about 20 percent of the total gross national product.

This direct government involvement in business activity was a source of debate between those who rejected any government economic activity, except for some essential services, and those who maintained that the government should engage in business activity to the largest possible extent.

These two approaches derive from opposing social ideologies; neither is compatible with economic efficiency. In fact, it is necessary to examine the government's business activity in the light of what it does for efficiency. Direct government involvement in business activity is one of the means by which the government can improve economic efficiency. Government intervention, however, should be limited to activities which do, in fact, contribute to higher efficiency. This may be so in the case of natural monopolies, or in activities with substantial externalities.

While government business activity is fundamentally the same as in the private sector, there is an essential difference in the *objectives* motivating it. Private firms operate on the basis of maximizing *profits,* while government operates on the basis of achieving maximum *welfare* for society. Where achieving maximum profits automatically insures the achievement of maximum welfare,

*151*

there is no need for government intervention. When these two aims are not compatible, there is room for intervention. It follows, therefore, that *profit cannot be a measure of the success of government business activity*. However, this conclusion is neither acceptable to the authorities who determine government policy nor to the administrators of government bodies. Government business organizations are too often guided by the search for profits; the majority of them are tempted to operate like monopolies, and thus harm the efficiency of the economy. Even the public, too, often equates the success of government business activity with profits, and thereby reaches wrong conclusions.

Here are some examples of distortion in the economic policies of government firms.

**Pricing of Telephone Service.**   Telephone service is a natural monopoly. In order to obtain economic efficiency (which is necessary for maximum welfare) the price must be set at a level equal to the marginal cost. If the marginal cost is lower than the average cost, economic efficiency requires the telephone service to operate at a loss, which must be offset by a government subsidy. This loss is not due to administrative inefficiency, nor is it a "waste of public funds"; it is, rather, a means for achieving efficient economic behavior.

In Israel, the telephone service is not operated this way but as a monopoly seeking to maximize profits by raising prices above the marginal cost, and even above the average cost. Indeed these profits go to the government instead of lining the pockets of a private individual but the economy's efficiency is damaged because of nonutilization to the fullest possible extent of telephone service, and by the inadequate level of existing communication services.

**Charter Flights.**   In 1963 charter flights to Israel were banned. This decision was made under strong pressure by El Al, the government airline. The airline was, indeed, interested in the weakening of foreign competition, thereby increasing its own income and profits.

The banning of charter flights harmed tourism to Israel and the income of the tourist branches of the economy. The issue should have been examined from the viewpoint of the entire economy: Was the income lost to the country by the absence of charter flights greater or less than the additional income gained by the airline? The answer to this question should have determined the government's decision.

**Israel Railways' Freight Rates.**   In negotiations conducted between the Dead Sea Works (a government corporation producing potash) and Israel Railways (a government departmental enterprise), each side tried to increase its profits at the expense of the other. The railway charged high haulage fees and the Dead Sea Works reasoned that such costs would damage its competitive export position on the foreign market. In such situations, the party able to muster the greatest government support usually wins. Let us assume that the government accepted the Dead Sea Works' argument and reduced the haulage fees to a level lower than the real marginal expenditure. On the face of it the Dead Sea Works would make a profit, since its accounts would show only its nominal expenditure for transporting its product. However, what is relevant are the real costs of transporting potash by train from the plant to the port; if these costs are higher the economy carries the full cost, irrespective of the figures in the Dead Sea Works' balance sheet.

There is frequent criticism that Israel Railways operates at a loss. It seems that this claim refers to administrative inefficiency. Be it right or wrong, the claim itself may be misleading because lack of profits is not a measure of inefficiency in a government enterprise. If its purpose was to obtain maximum profit, Israel Railways would have to behave like a monopoly and set its rates higher than its marginal costs. However, by doing so, Israel Railways would impair overall economic efficiency. The right criterion for evaluation of the managerial efficiency of railways as a business enterprise must be a direct assessment of its management. The evaluation of its economic efficiency should refer to its pricing policy, that is, whether its rates are equal to the corresponding marginal costs.

### Unclear Definition of Goals

Unclear definition of the goals of government enterprises often causes conflicts on insignificant issues which are irrelevant to the economy. These conflicts divert time and attention from the real issue of efficiency. Such a lack of clarity is exemplified by the legal dispute between the Industrial Development Bank and the income tax authorities, a dispute over the payment of income tax on linkage charges received by the bank for loans it granted. These linkage charges represented price-level adjustments of the loan principal.

The Industrial Development Bank (IDB) is, for all practical purposes, a government corporation. A significant portion of its capital comes from the government, with the remainder from other sources, in accordance with government terms. The terms of the loans given by IDB to industry are also set by the government. IDB's profits are thus dependent on both the interest it pays to its sources of funds, including that part provided by the government, and the interests it charges industry. If income tax payments on linkage differentials caused the bank to take a loss, the government would come to its aid by way of subsidies (which actually constitute tax rebates). If the nonpayment of income taxes brought special profits to the bank, the government would raise the interest rate on additional capital it provides to the bank. The conflict thus arises on an irrelevant and indeed insignificant issue—the transfer of funds from one government institution to another. Moreover, it is not, in fact, even an actual transfer, since in any case it will be offset by other measures bringing the bank to the same position whether the income tax was paid or not. This conflict developed into a court case only because of the ambiguity in the definition of the goals and objectives of government enterprises.

# Chapter Twenty-two

# Planning In Israel

In Chapter 8 we discussed the role of planning in the organization of economic activity. We saw that the most efficient economic organization is that which properly combines administration and market mechanisms, each operating where its contribution to economic efficiency is greater than the other's would have been.

In Israel we have, indeed, seen the operation of administration side by side with market and price mechanism. Moreover, it seems that the economic leadership in Israel has demonstrated sufficient freedom from ideological influences to be able to combine effectively the different means and methods for achieving its objectives.[a] There exists, however, a lack of clarity with respect to the exact spheres in which different means are most efficient, and how these should be integrated. We do not find a proper combination of planning and price mechanism; instead we find a mix that does not insure economic efficiency.

## The Legal System

Israel's legal system, on which the functioning of the market mechanism is based, is founded principally on British law inherited from the Mandate period. This law guarantees the principle of private ownership, and sets the legal framework of the commercial system, the monetary system, and so on. It thus created the conditions required for normal functioning of the price mechanism. However, the situation is somewhat more complicated owing to two factors.

First, the legal system also includes some ingredients of Ottoman law, including ideological elements that disturb efficient operation of the market. These elements are found, for example, in laws pertaining to land ownership and

---

[a]It is often difficult to distinguish between the various goals of government policy: which activities are intended to deal with externalities, which to cater to social preferences and which to benefit special interest groups.

the setting of interest rates. The Ottoman Law of Interest, for example, which was founded on traditional opposition to usury, constituted the basis for the 1957 Israel Law of Interest. In addition, Israel's own legislation, generally modern and efficient, is also not entirely free of ideology that damages economic efficiency. The first version of the Law for Encouraging Capital Investments prescribed that foreign capital invested voluntarily in Israel could not be freely withdrawn. This, and similar restrictions were, however, removed over the years.

The second complication in Israel's legal system is its reliance on the emergency laws imposed by the British Mandate during World War II. Temporary "Defense Laws" which regulate international commerce and foreign exchange have become "permanent," providing the government with instruments for intervention in the market, very often causing damage to efficiency (see chapters 13 and 15 on foreign trade and the capital market).

### Insuring Competitive Markets

Israel's government has at its disposal a large number of tools for regulating the level of competition in the market and thereby influencing its efficiency. We shall discuss several of these tools, indicating the nature of their influence.

The Business Restrictions Law was designed to provide the government with the power to prevent the development of monopolies and thus to improve market competitiveness and efficiency. And, indeed, the Israeli government employs these laws; but often it is for the opposite purpose. The government takes advantage of its authority specifically to *encourage* restrictive agreements. If such business practices were allowed on the condition that the domestic supply of their products is not reduced and thus that prices are kept at levels equal to the marginal cost, then efficiency would not be impaired. However, in most cases such restrictive agreements raised the price on the local market, using the profits to encourage export. We have already indicated the inefficiency of this method.

The Price Offices that operated in the years 1962–1965 and 1971–1972 were administrative bodies designed to influence the market. In order to improve efficiency, a price office had to assist in equalizing price to the marginal cost of the product. Thus, for example, it should have prevented monopolistic price rises to levels higher than marginal cost. However, since its policy was to postpone any price rises, it often created excess demand. This interference with the market mechanism damaged efficiency.

The price-control policy of 1949–1952 is another example of administrative intervention that impairs efficiency. However, the policy of lowering protective tariffs on import substitutes improves the level of efficiency if it reduces the effective rate-of-exchange differentials on imports.

If we add to the above examples additional administrative intervention in determination of prices for land, capital and foreign currency, we should conclude that, on balance, administrative intervention damaged rather than strengthened competition and efficiency.

### Setting Price Policy

In Israel administrative intervention is applied in the price determination of a great number of industries, including, of course, natural monopolies and goods and services with external advantages and disadvantages. The government, for example, exerts influence on setting prices for education, telephone service, electricity, water, train and bus fares, and so on. Such administrative intervention in the market mechanism will improve economic efficiency if, for example, natural monopolies are made to set their prices to equal their marginal cost. We have seen that in Israel, intervention is often guided by other considerations. Thus, for instance, discrimination in water prices is an inefficient means for subsidizing agriculture; and the telephone service charges are determined by the government, making use of its monopolistic power, to increase profits rather than to improve economic efficiency.

Much of the economic intervention of the Israeli government can be explained by social objectives. This is reflected in policies of price setting and administrative control. These policies are used not only to achieve overall social goals as maintained by the government but also in order to benefit specific groups.

Included among the overall objectives are: encouraging immigration, by rebating tariffs on import of their households and providing them with housing; encouraging Israeli students who have gone to other countries to return, by offering them conditions similar to those for immigrants; encouraging population-dispersion by subsidizing housing in development areas, by tax incentives to those who settle in such areas and by providing special benefits to investors in these areas.

Other measures for achieving general objectives are tax concessions on savings and special benefits to encourage investment. Also included within this framework are the taxing at a relatively high rate of nonpreferential products, such as luxuries, alcoholic beverages, and so on.

Direct administrative intervention for social goals is primarily directed at determining the composition of defense expenditures (with many details later set by the price mechanism). Direct intervention is also employed in legislation against drug abuse and the like.

Intervention in the price mechanism for the benefit of preferred groups is a very common practice. Low rent for both agricultural and urban land, low water charges for agricultural use, low interest rates on loans, special easy terms on short-term credit to agriculture and industry, laws protecting tenants from increasing housing rents, protective tariffs on specific products—these are among the items in the long list of special prices for the benefit of special groups, which damage the economy's efficiency.

Central administration can also assist special interest groups indirectly, such as by preventing entry of new competitors into certain industries and branches, such as taxi service, tourism, transportation, and others.

### Full Employment and Price Stability

Although the Israeli authorities have at their disposal adequate administrative means for achieving full employment and economic stability, they have not made good use of them. As we saw in Chapter 18, inflation was not successfully curbed; and when the balance-of-payments deficit increased, the deflationary measures taken brought recession and unemployment.

### Informational Planning

In the field of informational planning there has been substantial progress. A great number of departments, agencies and authorities were established and developed which conduct research in many spheres of economic activity and provide information to the public.

### Indicative Planning

Indicative planning is based on two fundamental principles: coordination and persuasion. Because of its significant economic involvement, the Israeli government has the power to assign directives to the various industries, sectors and even to individual firms. During the 1950s, when the Ministry of Commerce and Industry was interested in developing the textile industry, it not only offered to provide the capital resources needed, but actively selected a group of small industrialists and directed and persuaded them to raise this capital for its investments. In doing so it used various types of encouragement and incentives, sometimes even peculiarly ad hoc.[b]

Indicative planning seems to be of special importance in relations between the government and financial institutions. The largest financial groups very often are instruments for executing government programs. Their dependence on government favors insures their cooperation in the government's programs.

The government has at its disposal sufficient means of persuasion, which it utilizes through direct intervention in economic activity. These means are not necessarily formal. However, they often suffer from lack of coordination among government offices and organizations and from lack of long-range planning to define objectives and to designate the means by which these objectives can be achieved. This causes great damage to efficiency. If *coordination* is the main principle of indicative planning, then such planning is virtually nonexistent in Israel.

[b]For example, a specific small area in the industrial center of the city of Haifa, set aside for a specific plant, was legally defined as a "development area," enjoying thereby special economic privileges.

### Overt Government Enterprise Activity

The government operates as an independent concern in many areas (see Chapter 21). Especially significant is its activity as an owner of natural monopolies and of a business organization that provides products which have external effects. Such activities could indeed be regulated by means of the price mechanism. But the choice of regulation, by either the price mechanism or administration, must, in every instance, be made on the basis of efficiency. As we saw above, there is often a lack of clarity in the objectives of government companies. In their attempts to maximize profits these corporations may damage efficiency either by reduction of output (as is the case with natural monopolies), or by disregarding the external effects of their activities.

### Central Administration

While indicative planning is based on persuasion, central administration operates on compulsory directives. Central administration, which is employed in the socialist countries of Eastern Europe, can also be found in Israel, with agriculture constituting the outstanding example.

Central administration in agriculture is performed by the Central Planning and Development of Agriculture and Settlement under the auspices of the Ministry of Agriculture and the Jewish Agency. The aim of agricultural planning is "to establish agricultural policy for production, marketing, prices, and credits."[1]

Central administration in agriculture covers a vast area of activities. It determines quotas and prices for land and water for every agricultural unit, as well as production quotas and maximum and minimum prices on most of the agricultural products. The central administration operates through production and marketing committees that have legal authority over all the producers within their specific branches. The introduction of central administration in agriculture was justified by the inherent instability of agricultural price and output:

> There should have been an organization designed to protect the farmer from losses due to severe price fluctuations resulting in instability of production. On the other hand, an organization of this type is also essential for protecting the consumer from extreme price rises resulting from a reduction in supplies that usually follows price reductions.[2]
>
> The general purpose of price policy should be the improvement of resource allocation in the economy, with farmers' incomes increasing to the level stated in the plan.[3]

The Center for Agricultural Planning and Development operates as a large cartel, allocating production quotas to the different producers (farmers) and dividing the market among them. This cartel has the authority to impose its decisions on the farmers and to influence market prices. While the cartel can be effective in increasing farmers' incomes, it may damage economic efficiency. While the aim of restricting output is to increase prices, the individual farmer is interested in *increasing* his own output. But since the Center restricts the allocated land to each kind of agricultural product, the farmer can increase his output only by overintensive use of other outputs, principally water. This impairs economic efficiency in production.

The Center for Agricultural Planning and Development was, indeed, very successful in the introduction of new technological methods for increasing agricultural productivity. But this task can be fulfilled independently of central administration.

Central administration in Israel can also be found in other areas, such as the public services. Permission to operate transport systems must be obtained from the Ministry of Transportation. Any alterations in bus routes, the opening of new routes, changes in the frequency of bus stops, the setting of bus fares—all require permission from the responsible government authorities.

Control over a wide range of resources provides the government with the authority to transmit its directives through channels not necessarily within the official framework. An outstanding example is the government control of the capital market. First the government operates as a financial institution, receiving loans from various sources and providing direct loans to firms. Over the years the government has also established financial institutions that operate in accordance with its own instructions and private-sector financial institutions are also "coordinated" by the government. Thus the government's activities in the capital market are conducted through several administrative channels: indicative planning, direct administration and central administration.

Control of the capital market, enforced by a system of laws and regulations, provides the government with effective strength which, in practice, is exerted on the various economic sectors. Thus the government employs central administration not only in the agricultural sector (where the administration is official), but also in manufacturing and other industries. It is difficult to imagine a firm not getting permission, encouragement, and the benefits provided by the government, being able to enter the Israeli market and achieving a significant volume of output. In several notable cases the government itself instituted the establishment and development of new firms.

The car-assembly industry constitutes a clear example of central planning. An interoffice government committee often serves as a board of directors of existing firms. It authorizes investment and development programs for the firm, chooses new car models for assembly, provides permits for new firms to enter the industry, conducts transactions of transfer of ownership and determines the size and conditions of long-term loans to the firm.

The government also employs central administration in the building industry: the Ministry of Interior determines the uses of land, while the Ministry of Housing plans the various types of housing construction and the development of new neighborhoods and even new towns. The government participates in financing housing for newcomers, for low-income groups, for young couples, and so on.

All of these operations, in the form of central administration, cause damage to economic efficiency. We maintain that efficient planning requires proper integration of administration and market mechanism, so that each method can contribute its maximum to economic efficiency. Israel is a small country, and as the government has great economic influence, it can integrate administration with market mechanisms in a proper manner, serving as a model for other countries. The opportunity to do this has not yet been seized.

## NOTES

1. See *The Five Year Plan for Agricultural Development—1966/67–1970/71* (Tel Aviv: Center for Planning and Development of Agriculture and Settlements, 1966), p. 1.
2. *Report of the Public Committee for Investigating the Agricultural Situation in Israel,* Tel Aviv, 1960, p. 175.
3. *Five Year Plan,* loc. cit.

# Chapter Twenty-three

# The West Bank and the Gaza Strip: Economic Development

Israel's occupation of the West Bank was an unexpected result of the 1967 War. The area of the West Bank (2200 square miles) is about one-quarter that of Israel. It is bounded by Israel on the northwest and south, and by the Jordan River to the east. Its population in 1967 was over 800,000, declining to less than 600,000 with the emigration during and following the war.

The Gaza Strip, originally part of Palestine, was also occupied by Israel in 1967. Its land area is only about 150 square miles, located along the Mediterranean north of Sinai. It has a population of 360,000, most of them refugees from the 1948 War and their descendents. The density of population (2400 persons per square mile) is one of the highest in the world.

In this chapter we shall provide brief indications of the economic development of these territories since 1967, and in the next chapter we shall describe briefly and evaluate the main issues of economic policy in these territories.

### The Economic Setting: 1968

Both the West Bank and the Gaza Strip are underdeveloped areas, though the West Bank is relatively more developed. The 1967 War disturbed their economies only temporarily. Production was disrupted, unemployment widespread, some direct destruction was caused by the war and over 200,000 persons left the area for the East Bank of the Jordan. But in a few months most of the short-term disruptions were over.

By 1968 the economy was back to its prewar level of activity, allowing for the smaller population. A survey of the economy during 1968 gives us

Most of the data in this and the next chapter were provided by the Bank of Israel. We are deeply indebted to Mr. A. Bergman for his devoted help and for his comments on a draft of these two chapters. Also, see *The Economy of the Administered Areas,* 1969, 1970, 1971, 1972, Bank of Israel, Jerusalem.

appropriate information on prewar economic activity and provides a benchmark for reviewing its economic development under the Israeli regime.[a]

In 1968, the GNP of the West Bank amounted to $120 million.[b] With an average population of 585,000 this was $210 per capita. In the Gaza Strip the GNP was $50 million, the population 360,000 and the GNP per capita was $140. The opportunities for economic development in the West Bank were greater than in the Gaza Strip. The population in the West Bank was mostly rural (71 percent living in nonurban settlements). In the Gaza Strip about half the population were living in refugee camps, whereas only 9 percent of the West Bank population were in such camps.

Participation of the population in the labor force was very low, some 15 percent in the West Bank and 12 percent in the Gaza Strip. This is partly due to the age structure, since close to 50 percent of the population was below 14 years of age. However, the participation rate of the population of working age was also small, an indication of widespread, sometimes hidden, unemployment.

The main employment was in agriculture (35 percent in the West Bank and 26 percent in the Gaza Strip). Employment in services was relatively high, reflecting the unavailability of other employment opportunities. Manufacturing industry was underdeveloped, with some 13 percent of the employees engaged primarily in handcrafts. Building trades employed 10 percent of the employees. This employment structure was reflected also in the composition of the output. Services accounted for about 50 percent of the GNP, agriculture 37 percent, manufacturing 8 percent and construction about 5 percent each. Both the West Bank and the Gaza Strip had a deficit in the current account of their balance of payments. Exports consisted primarily of agricultural products. Before 1967, the export of services was more important than in 1968. This was in the form of services to tourists to the West Bank and work for the Egyptian Army in the Gaza Strip. The total deficit in the balance of payments amounted to some 25 percent of the GNP. In 1968, the loss of income from the export of services was covered by unilateral transfers from the Israeli government.

Before 1967 the rate of growth of the economies of the West Bank and the Gaza Strip had been very low. Since the Jordanian government concentrated its development efforts in the East Bank, and the Egyptian military regime did not encourage growth in the Gaza Strip, the level of employment was low, the per-capita income very low, and the standard of living depressed. The economies depended on the foreign aid provided by the United Nations' help to the refugees (UNRWA), and by private transfers from relatives, particularly young Palestinians who acquired professions and found jobs in other countries. The structure of the economies was also typical of an underdeveloped area, with a

---

[a]This survey does not include East Jerusalem, which was officially annexed to Israel in 1967 and on which no separate data are available.

[b]All the data are quoted in dollars. The figures are adjusted to constant 1971 price level, and converted from Israeli pounds to dollars at the 1971 average official rate of exchange (IL 3.7 to $1).

low level of industry and higher levels of agriculture and services. In both the West Bank and the Gaza Strip the share of agriculture was smaller and that of services higher than for typical developing countries, reflecting the special features of the natural resources and the social and political environment.

### Economic Growth: 1968–1973

Since 1968 the economies of the West Bank and the Gaza Strip have grown at an unprecedented pace. The GNP in real terms increased at more than 16 percent per annum. Since the population grew only by 2 percent per annum, the real GNP per capita rose at an annual rate of 14 percent (see Table 23-1).

This rapid growth was a result of two major factors. The first was increasing job opportunities, which brought about a rapid increase in employment. While the population increased by only 12 percent, employment size rose by 54 percent, and the participation rate of population in the labor force increased from 16 percent to 19 percent.

The second major factor in the rapid growth was increased productivity. This was manifested primarily in agriculture. There was a significant change in the structure of agricultural production on the basis of relative advantages with regard to Israel. In addition, technological improvements were introduced. The Israeli Ministry of Agriculture organized training, and the farmers were very perceptive in accepting the improved technologies and crops. As a result the agricultural output (in real terms) in 1972 was 80 percent greater than in 1968, while the number of employees in agriculture declined. Thus the output per employee was doubled. Manufacturing industry also developed rapidly, but not faster than the economy as a whole. Productivity in the manufacturing industry increased by the acquisition of knowhow from Israeli industrial plants. Such plants (like textiles) subcontracted work to Arab industry.

A third but less significant factor in economic growth was capital investment. This amounted to very little in 1968, but increased rapidly, reaching 15 percent of the GNP in 1972. It is expected to become even more important in future economic growth.

The close economic interconnections between the territories and Israel is the ultimate source of this rapid economic growth. The Israeli economy provided markets for the increased output as well as the knowhow required for adopting the more highly productive technologies. But above all, the Israeli economy provided jobs for Arab employees. The number of such employees living within the territories and working in Israel increased rapidly, reaching over 60,000 in 1973, about one-third of the total employees. Over 50 percent were employed in the Israeli building industry and about 18 percent in agriculture, the rest being equally divided between services (12 percent) and manufacturing (18 percent). On the whole, these employees constituted a cheap labor force for Israel, though their real wage increased rapidly and was much higher than the wage paid for similar jobs in the territories.

Employment opportunities in Israel not only helped to eliminate

**Table 23-1. Population and Gross National Product in the West Bank and the Gaza Strip: 1968–1973 (in 1971 prices)**

| | Population (thousands) | | | Gross National Product (million $) | | | GNP per Capita ($) | | |
|---|---|---|---|---|---|---|---|---|---|
| | West Bank | Gaza Strip | Total | West Bank | Gaza Strip | Total | West Bank | Gaza Strip | Total |
| 1968 | 580 | 360 | 940 | 120 | 50 | 170 | 200 | 130 | 180 |
| 1969 | 595 | 360 | 955 | 150 | 55 | 205 | 250 | 150 | 210 |
| 1970 | 605 | 370 | 975 | 165 | 70 | 235 | 270 | 190 | 240 |
| 1971 | 620 | 380 | 1000 | 200 | 80 | 280 | 320 | 220 | 280 |
| 1972 | 630 | 385 | 1015 | 250 | 100 | 350 | 395 | 260 | 345 |
| 1973 | 650 | 400 | 1050 | 235 | 115 | 350 | 365 | 285 | 335 |
| Annual rate of growth | 2.4% | 2.0% | 2.2% | 14.5% | 19.4% | 16.0% | 11.8% | 17.0% | 13.5% |

Source: Research Department, Bank of Israel (figures slightly rounded).

unemployment in the territories but also made possible increased productivity and output. That total employment would have been lower in the absence of these employment opportunities is a reasonable assumption, judging from the high savings rate of the increment of national income, which was invested mainly in liquid assets. The rate of savings of the increment of the net income between 1968 and 1972 was over 26 percent, increasing the average rate of saving from 11 to 23 percent.

### Foreign Trade and the Balance of Payments

Foreign trade grew even more rapidly than the GNP. Total imports increased from $90 million in 1968 to $280 million in 1972, and exports rose from $50 million to $260 million. The deficit in the current account of the balance of payments consequently declined from $40 million to $20 million.

The main export was that of labor services provided by Arab employees to Israel proper. This item which did not exist in 1967, gradually increased and reached $150 million in 1973. Most of the export of goods consisted of agricultural products, and this more than doubled between 1968 and 1972. The main increase was in export to Israel, but export to Jordan also constituted a substantial part of the total. Imports increased rapidly, too, mainly in the form of industrial products from Israel.

Unilateral transfers from private sources did not change much, and reached only $30 million in 1972. A similar sum was granted by the Israeli government. As a result, foreign reserves were being accumulated in the hands of the people, primarily in the form of cash.

### The Monetary System and the Price Level

The monetary system of the territories is underdeveloped. The share of demand deposits in the total money supply was, and remained, only 10 percent. There was a trend to hold a substantial part of savings in cash, in the form of Jordanian dinars. The total money supply increased from $60 million at the end of 1967 to $190 million at the end of 1972. The price level was affected by the inflation in Israel. In 1968 and 1969 the price level was quite stable (both in Israel and in the territories). But after 1970 there was a rapid rate of price increase: 8 percent in 1970, 18 percent in 1971 and 18 percent in 1972, and 22 percent in 1973.

### Conclusion

The progress and prosperity of the West Bank and the Gaza Strip since 1967 was achieved primarily by increased productivity and tight economic relationships with Israel and less by capital imports. Government economic policy played a crucial role in making this development possible. In the next chapter we review the main characteristics of the economic policy applied in the territories and show how it contributed to this outstanding rate of economic growth.

# Chapter Twenty-four

# The West Bank and the Gaza Strip: Economic Policy

After the West Bank and the Gaza Strip were taken over in 1967, a key and urgent economic question was raised: Should the territories be kept isolated from the Israeli economy (as they had been up to then) and developed as a closed, independent economic system; or should they be integrated into the Israeli economy? The political background, as seen by the Israeli government, was consistent with a policy of economic integration. It was widely accepted that under a final, peaceful settlement of the political conflict, the territories might very well be under a non-Israeli regime (either an independent state or part of Jordan). However, since it was assumed that such development could take place only in the context of a peaceful political solution, close economic relations between Israel and the territories would be retained. Therefore, a policy of encouraging economic integration during the period of the Israeli occupation was regarded as consistent with any peaceful political solution. On the basis of this consideration the decision was made to develop close economic interconnections between Israel and the territories.

Another key policy decision had to do with the nature of the Israeli military regime. The decision was to follow a policy of minimum intervention in local and internal life and politics, reserving controls primarily to defense and foreign affairs. This was a purely political decision but it had far-reaching economic policy implications, since it meant refraining from detailed intervention in internal economic activities. This resulted in a quite peculiar situation: while in Israel the government had been deeply involved in economic and business activity, even on the micro level, the territories enjoyed much greater freedom.

The third key policy problem had to do with the economic relationships between the West Bank and the Arab countries, particularly Jordan. From 1949 to 1967 the West Bank was part of the state of Jordan and had close economic relations with the East Bank. Long-term political considerations led Israel to allow the continuation of normal economic relations between the two

*169*

Banks. This resulted in the policy of so-called "open bridges," according to which there was a free physical flow of goods between the two territories, over the Jordan bridges. This decision could not have been implemented without the (unofficial) cooperation of the Jordanian government.

These three major decisions determined the main economic policy decisions, with regard to the territories, as reviewed below.

### Integration with the Israeli Economy

The policy of increasing economic ties between the territories and Israel was manifested in several areas.

**Free Trade.**   Obstacles to the exchange of goods and services were removed quite rapidly. A few months after the occupation the borders were opened to free transfer of goods without any administrative control[a] and no tariffs imposed on this trade. (In order to avoid unfavorable repercussions and to equalize conditions with Israel, a tariff was imposed on all imports to the territories from the rest of the world, including Jordan, at Israeli rates.) In addition, excise taxes, sales taxes, and income taxes—and all other taxes imposed in Israel—were extended to the territories. The result was that for all practical purposes of internal and foreign trade, Israel and the territories became one common market. This allowed free trade between the economies under homogeneous conditions.

**Free Movement of the Labor Force.**   The Israeli government allowed, and as a matter of fact actively encouraged, the free movement of manpower. This turned out to be a one-way street—from the territories to Israel. With full employment restored in Israel in 1969, and unemployment in the territories, this was the natural direction. Since distances between the population centers in the territories and employment centers in Israel are short, it was possible for most of the employees to travel from home to work every day. The Israeli government facilitated this development by gradual cancellation of all kinds of administrative requirements involved in this movement. Thus, the required official permits that had been installed after the war, and applied to both sides, were gradually cancelled, first with regard to Israeli citizens, later with regard to the West Bank and finally for the Gaza Strip. In addition, the Ministry of Labor provided administrative help and information to Israeli employers and Arab employees in order to facilitate the process of finding jobs and travelling to and from them.

---

[a]There was, however, one exception: pressure from Israeli farmers caused the government to control the export to Israel of some agricultural products. This impaired economic efficiency. However, over the years a process of adjustment did take place, and some of these controls were removed.

**A Common Monetary System.** A short time after the war the Israeli and the territorial monetary systems were integrated in the following way. The Israeli pound became an official currency in the territories, with free exchange to the Jordanian dinar. The dinar, however, also remained as a second (but not secondary) official currency. Thus, despite the exchange control in Israel, citizens of the territories are free to hold dinars side-by-side with Israeli currency.

This unification of the monetary system with a free exchange of Israeli pounds to dinars made the monetary integration effective and efficient. The free exchange of dinars was particularly important, because it removed, to a great extent, the potential reluctance of the Arabs to using the Israeli pound. And indeed, in the first years, a pattern was created: use of the Israeli pound for transactions, and the dinar for hoarding. Later, as of 1971, a significant change was noticed, and most of the incremental savings in money is now made in the form of Israeli pounds.

**Other Measures.** Two other important conditions that contributed to economic integration were free capital transfers and the free movement of knowhow and technology.

The free transfer of capital made it possible for Israelis to invest in economic ventures in the territories. Because of the politically uncertain future, this kind of activity did not develop to any significant extent.

The Israeli government did encourage the transfer of technology and knowhow. Thus, the Ministry of Agriculture organized a drive to introduce more advanced methods in agriculture. Industrial firms were encouraged to provide knowhow to their subcontractors, a system that became widely spread in several industries, especially textiles, confection, furniture and some foodstuffs.

These policy measures proved to be very effective in integrating the economies. This is clear from the survey of the economic development of the territories in the previous chapter. Here we briefly summarize the main developments of this integration.

Trade with Israel increased very rapidly. By 1973 export of goods to Israel constituted 60 percent of the total export, and import of goods from Israel was 90 percent of the total import. Most of the import of services was from Israel. Export of services to Israel was mainly in the form of labor from the territories working in Israel. This was the most important economic development. The total number of such employees in Israel in 1972 was more than 50,000, constituting about *one-third* of the total number of territory employees. Their total income (in the form of export of services) reached $85 million, that is, about one-third of the total GNP. The total export (of goods and services) to Israel amounted to 65 percent of the GNP, and the total import from Israel was somewhat higher.

This development took place both in the West Bank and in the Gaza

Strip. In the latter, the process follows the pattern set by the West Bank with a time lag of about one year.

There was great concern in Israel about the high movement of labor. It became disturbing, because the Arabs are employed in nonprofessional, non-skilled, low-wage jobs. This has unfavorable social and political repercussions. With this in mind the Israeli government decided, in 1972, to put some limits on "excessive" Arab employment in Israel. The wage level in Israel has been higher than in the territories by about 40 percent. It seems that this gap will persist also in the future, because the Israel wage level is rising rapidly. Thus there was great incentive to work in Israel, and only in the long term, when there will be greater capital investment and technological progress in the territories and the wage level there rises rapidly too, will the pattern change toward a smaller wage differential and a lower relative employment in Israel. If this develops, it seems that any political change that ends the Israeli regime in the territories but retains peaceful and friendly political relations will not affect the economically close relations, which in such a political environment can be further developed in an official "common market" framework.

### Government Intervention

Because of the military regime's policy of noninvolvement in the internal affairs of the territories, Israel's government was careful not to intervene in internal economic activity. Thus, development of agriculture, industry and various services continued under a free environment, more so than in the Israel economy.

In the early years of the occupation, when unemployment in the territories was high and work in Israel not yet widespread, the Israel government provided financing for public works, which eased unemployment somewhat. After 1969 this activity diminished relative to the overall level of employment.

### The "Open Bridges"

The policy of open bridges allowed for the continuation of trade relations with the Arab countries, via Jordan. This was a very important step in restoring economic activity to a normal level after the disruption of the 1967 War. It provided market outlets for agricultural crops and prevented an economic crisis. However, with the development of free trade with Israel and the imposition of the Israeli tariffs on trade with the rest of the world, the relative advantage in this trade diminished. Thus, while the export of goods via the open bridges amounted to 50 percent of total exports in the early period, it gradually declined, and in 1973 it amounted to only 20 percent. The import of goods from Jordan was always small, gradually declining from 8 percent of total imports in 1968 to 5 percent in 1972.

The Jordanian government cooperated with this policy because it was anxious to retain its previous ties with the West Bank. It therefore also continued paying salaries to its employees who remained in the West Bank and continued doing their jobs, particularly in internal services (law, education and so on). The Israeli government permitted this transfer of salaries, which constituted an additional source of income. In 1972 the Jordanian government reduced these payments as a result of changes in its policy with regard to the West Bank.

### Evaluation of the Economic Policy

The introduction of the free flow of goods, services, labor, capital and technology between Israel and the territories, with neither administrative barriers nor price differentials, made it possible for both economies to adjust to each other by specializing in economic activities with relative advantages. This contributed to an increase in the economic efficiency of both economies. Indeed, the total effect on the Israeli economy was minor, because of its greater size, but the effect on the economic structure of the territories was very significant. This is manifested by changes that took place in the structure of agricultural and industrial output. In general the territories increased the output of labor-intensive activities in field crops and vegetables, as well as in textiles, foodstuffs, building materials, handcrafts and light industry. The free movement of labor made it possible virtually to eliminate unemployment and to absorb the additional labor set free from domestic production by increased productivity.

Indeed, the imposition of the Israeli price structure on the territories resulted in the introduction of all kinds of distortions which persist in the Israeli economy. This might hamper economic efficiency. The resulting damage was not necessarily borne by the territories, but often by Israel itself. For example, subsidization of the import of basic commodities to Israel made them available to the territories at prices lower than they would have paid otherwise. And since this policy was designed to assist the low-income groups, the territories benefited from it.[b]

It thus seems that the policy of integrating the economies of the territories with Israel was a decisive factor in accelerating the growth and progress of these economies.

Given the excessive intervention of the Israeli government in the Israeli economy, its lower level of intervention in the economies of the territories created better conditions to achieve economic efficiency and also contributed to rapid economic growth.

On the other hand, the government could have done more than it actually did to encourage capital investments in the territories. Despite the high level of saving, investment remained low, probably because of the uncertainty of the political future. The Israeli government was not active enough in overcoming this obstacle. It could have helped in creating local financial institutions

---

[b]There were even cases where the subsidized commodities were smuggled to Jordan and sold at international market prices.

that would mobilize internal resources and invest them in development. It could
have encouraged Israeli capital investments by providing political insurance. And
above all, it could—and should have— encouraged international financial institutions to invest in the territories as part of a massive development program
to help solve the refugees' economic problems, particularly pressing in the Gaza
Strip.

The "open bridges" policy, which was essentially a politically
induced step, contributed favorably to economic development. Its importance
was particularly notable in the early period of the occupation.

One should not overlook the difficulties and obstacles to economic
development of the territories that resulted from the political uncertainty. This
uncertainty disrupted the otherwise smooth and rapid economic growth and
progress. The 1973 War, for example, demonstrated clearly such unfavorable
potential development. However, the economic development during the period
1968-1973 shows how efficient economic policy can contribute to economic
growth, helping to achieve rates of economic growth per capita greater than any-
where else, even in the face of political uncertainty.

## Chapter Twenty-five

# General Conclusion:
# Economic Policy, Efficiency
# and Growth in Israel

The economic growth of the Israeli economy is indeed impressive. Within 22 years total domestic output increased in real terms eight times, and the real income per capita 2.3 times. The question which remains to be answered is: What was the contribution of economic policy in Israel to this growth? We have seen that economic policy can encourage growth in two main ways, not necessarily in conflict.

The first is by increasing the efficiency of the economy as a whole. This would result in greater resources that could be applied to raising the level of achievement of any goal without sacrificing any other goal. And since economic growth is one of the main goals and most decisive for the very existence of the state of Israel, it follows that increasing economic efficiency can provide greater resources for increasing the rate of economic growth.

The second way to increase the rate of growth is by diverting more resources from private and public consumption to investment. This is, of course, a more "expensive" way, since it comes at the expense of other goals.

Of the two ways, increasing efficiency is the more important, as explained in the introduction. The performance of economic policy in Israel and its contribution to economic growth has to be tested not against actual growth, impressive as it was, but against the level of growth that could have been achieved without hurting the level of achievement of other goals. Thus the success of the economic policy must be tested by its contribution to economic efficiency.

In line with these considerations, this concluding chapter is divided into three parts. First we deal with the contribution of economic policy to the efficiency of the Israel economy; then we examine the effect of this policy on the allocation of resources between investment and consumption, and finally we summarize our conclusions.

### Economic Efficiency

The rapid growth of Israel's economy is explained primarily by the increase in the tangible production factors—labor and capital. As we have seen in Chapter 12, these factors account for about two-thirds of the growth. The remaining third comes from increased productivity—a rather significant figure. However, we believe that the main reason for this increase in productivity is not because of greater economic efficiency but through increased technological and managerial efficiency.

This belief derives from the fact that over the period under review there was a substantial increase in the level of education and the professional skill of the labor force, and that modern methods of production, operation and organization were introduced. All these were manifested in the increased productivity of the economy.

There still remains the question of whether economic policy also contributed to this increase in productivity, through increased economic efficiency. Here we have to differentiate between two aspects of the question: (1) Was the policy efficient?; and (2) if the policy was not efficient, was there any significant improvement in the efficiency of the policy in the course of time? This second question is relevant, since improving efficiency of the economic policy would, in time, contribute to increased economic productivity and thereby to its rate of growth.

The survey of economic policy in Israel in the preceding chapters shows quite a low level of economic efficiency. In foreign trade, the multiple effective exchange rates caused inefficient allocation of resources for production both between the local market and export, and within each group. We have seen that as a result the economy earns less foreign exchange than it could have earned had there been only one unified exchange rate for all the exports and imports.

The controlled prices distorted the structure of the price system. It discouraged the development of products with relative advantages and encouraged the development of products that are less worthwhile. As a result, total production was lower than it could have been.

The low interest rates on long-term investment capital encouraged investment in projects that did not yield the highest possible return, and also caused overinvestment in capital-intensive technologies. The administrative direction of short-term credit is bound to allocate it inefficiently.

The excessively low prices of water, combined with administrative allocation, did not insure maximum agricultural output from the given supply.

Income tax applied to a small income base at a very high rate distorted the wage structure, discouraged the desire to work and caused misallocation of labor. Indirect taxes, which were also levied on a small number of products at a very high rate, distorted the price structure and thereby created inefficiency similar to that resulting from price control.

We have also seen that the system of production and allocation of public services is far from efficient, either managerially or economically. The inflationary process also damaged economic efficiency, and government action against inflation—controlled prices, allocation of excessive subsidies to certain products, delay in adjusting the rate of exchange—all further impaired economic efficiency.

The deflationary policy deliberately introduced in the mid-1960s was inefficient, since it created unemployment and halted the growth of the economy while it achieved very little toward its avowed purposes: stopping the inflation and changing the employment structure to increase the production of exports and of import substitutes.

Economic policy in Israel, then, has obviously been inefficient. The second question remains: Was there any improvement in economic policy efficiency? It is hard to provide a substantiated answer to this question since such an answer would have to be based on accurate estimates of the relative importance of the different components of economic policy. Generally, however, it seems that in different areas and at different times efficiency of the policy fluctuated, with no clear trend emerging.

In the beginning of the 1950s, the period of controls, rationing and suppressed inflation, economic policy was not efficient. The economic policy of 1952 took steps to alleviate some inefficiencies but introduced new ones: increased unemployment and a reduced rate of economic growth. In the second half of the 1950s, with the suspension of direct controls on import quotas and the reduction in the rate of inflation, efficiency improved. At the same time, however, the range of multiple exchange-rates increased, and damaged efficiency. One should expect an improvement in efficiency with the economic policy of 1962, which was designed to unify the exchange rates. But this policy was never really implemented. The deflationary policy of the mid-1960s, which brought the recession, clearly damaged efficiency. The full employment policy, as of 1967, constituted an improvement in efficiency. But the increase in the burden of taxation, while reducing the base on which the taxes were imposed (a process that took place after 1967 and sharpened in 1970), damaged efficiency. Some corrections in the rate of exchange during the years 1970–1971 constituted an improvement in economic efficiency, but deepening inflation, due to increased government expenditures and the imposition of price controls in 1971, neutralized this favorable development. Increased importance and growth of public services was accompanied by increased waste and inefficiency. In other fields of economic policy, such as investment encouragement, low interest rates, direction of short-term credit, water-pricing, land-pricing, and wage policy, there were no significant changes in the efficiency. The growth in productivity must be attributed primarily to technological, managerial and human improvements in the production process and not to economic policy.

### Capital Formation

The rate of capital formation in Israel has been relatively high, favorably affecting the rate of economic growth. The questions to be discussed here are what the contribution of government policy to this development was, and particularly, how economic policy affected the efficiency of capital allocation. The answer to these questions are rather complex. Looking into the actual allocation of total resources (Chapter 12) one finds that the volume of net capital formation was not higher than the total capital import. Most of the time it was lower. This means that capital formation in Israel was, on a net basis, financed by capital import. In other words, most of the time the level of local saving was negative. As indicated above, there was some positive saving by families and the business sector, though not very high. However, the deficit in the government budget (that is, the government's negative saving), brought total saving down to about zero. In order to increase growth, one should encourage savings, thereby transferring resources from consumption to capital formation. This is the case only when aggregate demand in the economy is sufficient to provide full employment, but these conditions persisted in Israel during most of the period under discussion.

In order to increase total savings and capital formation, the government could cut its direct expenditures for public consumption; cut private consumption by increasing tax levies; and raise interest rates on savings in order to increase voluntary saving. However, it is questionable whether it would have been desirable to reduce the level of public consumption. During the years prior to 1968, it would have been possible to increase the burden of real taxation, had the tax structure been more efficient. This would have provided the government with resources and, therefore, with positive saving, greater than the reduction in saving of both the families and the business sector that would have followed. The main failure of government economic policy in this respect was its discouragement of voluntary private saving, by lowering interest rates paid to savers.

Being a major borrower in the capital market, the government was too concerned over the burden of interest it had to carry on its debt, and tried to lower its borrowing costs. For example, after the 1962 devaluation inflationary pressure accumulated. At that very time, the government *lowered* interest rates for savers purchasing its bonds, instead of raising rates. While the interest paid to savers is indeed a government expenditure, it is just one item in the list of such expenditures. It might be desirable for this item to take precedence over other types of expenditures that exert relatively less encouragement to growth and to public welfare. Erroneous government judgments as to the nature of the capital market led to a policy that discouraged savings, and government controls prevented market forces from neutralizing this damage.[1]

In order to compensate for the lower level of saving, the government encouraged capital formation in two ways; by increasing capital import and by inflationary finance. The government encouraged capital import by its policy of accepting any foreign loan available, even at quite high interest rates. In most years the government was ready to pay interest up to 8 percent per year, and in some years even higher. As a result capital import has indeed been higher than it would have been otherwise, and thereby has contributed to capital formation and growth. But the price paid was quite high. At the end of 1973 the Israeli economy was over $5 billion in debt, and therefore subject to substantial dangers regarding its ability to borrow in the future should unexpected needs, primarily for defense, appear. Moreover, this was an inefficient economic policy. The rates of interest on foreign loans which the government actually paid (reaching 8 percent) was higher than the 5.5 percent it paid to local savers in most years (6.5 percent in 1971 and 3 percent in 1974). These loans are linked to the price index, while foreign loans are linked to the foreign exchange rate. In addition, the government deducts a 25 percent income tax from these interest payments to local savers. It would, therefore, have been possible to increase economic efficiency by raising the interest rates to local savers and reducing the ceiling rate on foreign loans, equalizing them at a rate that still provides the same amount of capital.

The second way in which the government increased capital formation was inflationary financing. This method was utilized to a great extent during the early years of the state of Israel,[2] and continued in later years as well.

As a means of encouraging growth, inflationary financing is very popular, not only in Israel but in most developing countries. Due to structural and political factors, it is very difficult in such countries to transfer resources from the public to the government by taxation and loans. Hence the government seized on inflationary financing. Used as an instrument for transferring resources from consumption to investment, inflationary finance may result in the opposite, slowing down the rate of growth. Inflation can affect the growth rate because it harms the economy's efficiency.[3] Prices do not rise at an equal rate for all products. For social and political reasons governments often prevent price rises in certain industries (food, public transport, housing) by exerting price controls. These controls cause steeper price rises in industries not under control, which, in turn, encourages expansion in nonpreferred sectors of the economy. The government then must allocate its limited resources, which should finance investment, to supporting the price of the products. The emerging changes in the price structure cause distortion in the judgment of private consumers in determining their consumption patterns. Moreover, different rates of price rise in the different sectors raise uncertainty regarding future prices, further distorting producer and consumer decisions. In view of the uncertain future value of savings, the desire to save also diminishes. Inflation causes additional damage since the foreign exchange rate is often fixed, thus export profitability falls and import profitability rises. To overcome this difficulty, governments often levy protective tariffs and import quotas. Production of import substitutions then becomes overattractive, while production for export becomes less attractive. This causes a shift to import substitutes, which means an inefficient allocation of production factors. These developments occurred in Israel, too, though not to the same extent as in some other developing countries.

This discussion spells out the types of damage to economic growth caused by inflation. As long as prices rise at a slow rate the damage is not so marked; however, when prices rise more than 3–4 percent per annum, the damage increases severely. From 1948 to 1973 the consumer price index rose in Israel over seven times, averaging more than 8 percent per annum; and the index underestimates the average rate at which all prices rose throughout the entire period. Thus it is not clear at all that the inflation in Israel contributed anything to encourage economic growth.

The effect of government policy on capital formation is not limited to savings policy. It extends to the encouragement of investors to use available resources and make investments. The Israeli government, indeed, did much to encourage capital formation. It granted loans to investors quite easily, at low interest rates and over a long period and without linkage, despite the inflation. In some years the government also made special grants to investors—up to 20 percent of the investment in fixed assets. The Law for Encouragement of Capital Investment also provides special tax privileges on profits from approved investments (through accelerated depreciation and special, low income-tax rates). Moreover, there is no additional taxation, under this law, on profits distributed as dividends. Such encouragement has indeed contributed to the increase in capital investment and growth. However, the incentives themselves made for inefficiency (low interest rates encourage misallocation and waste of capital). Government policy, then, did not have a clearcut impact on allocation. Some of its measures damaged capital formation, while others encouraged it. However, even those that encouraged capital formation were economically inefficient; they achieved their goal while putting unnecessary burdens on the economy. Had these burdens been avoided by following a more efficient economic policy, higher rates of economic growth could have been achieved.

### Conclusion

Perhaps the main lesson to be learned from the history of Israel's economic progress is that neither austerity nor efficient utilization of the price mechanism played a major role in that progress. This is not to say that Israel's economic policy was *bad* in any general sense, as compared to the economic policies of governments elsewhere. It could very well have been much worse, resulting in less economic progress. What is significant is that there was no clear improvement in Israel's economic policy, and the country's splendid picture of economic growth was not a result of that policy. It was achieved despite the basic inefficiency of its economic organization and structure, characterized by excessive use of central administration and inappropriate use of price mechanisms.

Indeed, Israel has been relatively free both from the blinkers that once hindered the socialist countries in their attempts to administer the economy without a price mechanism, and from those that obstructed the capitalist countries, which rejected the delegation to their governments of even some central administrative authority (for example, for combating unemployment).

A small country, with a strong and influential government, Israel could have properly combined central administration and market mechanism and thereby become a model that both developing and developed countries could follow.

But Israel has not lived up to these expectations. One reason for its failure is the lack of understanding of the basic economic principles discussed in this book. Thus, many planners still support an excessive use of central administration, disregarding the advantages of making efficient use of the market mechanism; and many economists still place excessive reliance on the market mechanism, overlooking the benefits that can be derived from proper use of central administration.

But lack of understanding of the economic issues is probably not the only reason for failure; sociopolitical factors must be examined. For a system of central administration to be effective, a powerful economic bureaucracy is necessary. Such a bureaucracy naturally tends to conserve —and to increase—its power by repeating past administrative patterns and even overdoing them. It also tends to develop protective devices that automatically neutralize counterforces. The most important of these protective devices in the Israeli bureaucratic system is "personalism."

The personalism that pervades Israel's economy derives, in part, from the unwillingness of people to relinquish power—and perhaps the most attractive of all is the power to do favors for people. This, the more pleasant aspect of personalism, often expresses itself in personal intervention to overcome oppressive bureaucratic decisions that would ride roughshod over people's sensibilities and even their vital concerns. It is also in contrast to the heartlessness of the cash nexus. Finally, it has roots in the relative efficiency of invoking personal loyalties for the achievement of tasks where appropriate administrative or market mechanisms have not been adequately developed.

This last aspect is reflected in the frequency with which criticism of the market and of competition turns out to be criticism of an *insufficiency* of competition or of *incompetence* in the use of the market mechanism. In exactly the same way condemnations of bureaucracy, when examined more closely, turn out to be criticisms of an *insufficient* development of administrative techniques. In both cases, furthermore, the imperfections of the market or administrative system often stem from the same warm personalism that deprecates their coldness. The evils are the other side of the coin of the personal favors given, which inevitably involve the freezing out of the invisible men who have to wait longer, or even to go without, because of the favors given to others. It is the retention of the power to give favors that sabotages development of generally more efficient and more just—because more evenhanded—administrative and market mechanisms.

And yet, as long as the administrative and market mechanisms are imperfectly developed and not completely attuned to social objectives, there remains a legitimate place for personal intervention for the correction of the injustices and cruelties inevitable in the automatic working of these mechanisms. At the same time the exercise of such informal intervention hinders refinement of the mechanisms and even brings about retrogression and impairment, which make still more intervention necessary.

This vicious circle can be turned into a beneficial circle if the intervention on behalf of victims is itself organized in an impersonal manner. The contradiction necessarily inherent in an "impersonal personalism" is recognized as only *apparent* when it is realized that it is the *victims* that need to be considered and not the distributors of personal favors. Recognition that this is the nature of the problem is to be seen in the worldwide movement for the establishment of "ombudsmen"—an impartial and impersonal administrative mechanism—to correct administrative injustices. A similar tendency is to be seen in the growing interest in the replacement of the dispensation of benefits to losers in the *market* distribution of income by welfare agencies on an overly personal basis by an impersonal, because universally applicable, "social dividend" called "negative income tax."

Such regularization and impersonalization in the correction of inequities could do much toward the reduction of personalism, and thereby contribute to the greater development of market and administrative mechanisms. These, in turn, would weaken the urge for personalism, setting the stage for still further and more rapid overall improvement of the efficiency and equity of the economy.

Excessive government intervention and widespread "personalism" are the main reasons for Israel's economic inefficiency. They not only created inefficiencies, they also prevented the improvement of economic policy and prevented greater materialization of Israelis economic growth potential. The experience with the territories seems to support this argument. Here, for political reasons, the Israel Government avoided excessive economic intervention. As a result, its economic policy was probably more efficient, witness the significantly higher rate of economic growth in the territories. Had the economic policy in Israel followed similar principles, Israel proper would have seen a greater rate of economic growth, and could have constituted an outstanding example for other countries to follow.

## NOTES

1. When analyzing government economic policy in the field of saving during the period 1948–1958, Professor D. Patinkin came to the following conclusion: "The fact that the Israeli economy did not save a greater part of its national income, which has grown very fast, seems to be the main failure of the economic policy in Israel." See D. Patinkin, *Israel Economy – First Decade.* (Jerusalem: Falk Institute of Economic Search, 1965), p. 93.
2. In 1949 the government proposed to finance the development budget (the budget for investments) by printing money with a cover of Land Bills. The Minister of Finance at that time, Mr. E. Kaplan, promised the Israeli Knesset: "We have introduced into the Act a special regulation according to which we can allocate the funds raised by Land Bills only to basic investments, that is to investments which create real long-term fixed assets." See *Knesset Minutes*, Volume 16, p. 682.
3. See, for example, Harry G. Johnson, "Is Inflation the Inevitable Price of Rapid Development, or a Retarding Factor in Economic Growth?" Rehovoth Conference, 1965.

# Index

agriculture, 68, 79; exchange rates, 89; policy, 108; subsidy and water, 105
Arabs, 107; employment, 135
Austria, 117

balance-of-payments, 61, 68, 94; deficit, 136; West Bank and Gaza, 167
Bank of Israel, 132; tight money policy, 138
Belgium, 117
Berglas, E., 118
black market, 94
Britain, 146
Business Restrictions Law, 88; authority, 95; and monopoly, 156; price manipulation, 93

capital: accumulation, 74; allocation, 99; formation, 75, 178; transfer transactions, 89
cartels, 50, 88
centralization, 40, 140; and decisionmaking, 25
Central Planning and Development of Agriculture and Settlement, 159
Ceylon, 146
Committee for Investigating Land Policies, 107
commodities, 94, 122
consumption: balanced budget, 131, 132; and economic efficiency, 19 and economic policy, 175; intervention, 57; investment, 39; price rigidity, 50; private and rate of decline, 137; resources, 81; and utility, 11
consumer, 38
controls: and balance of payments, resource allocation, 96; and centralization, 48; government and banks, 100; government

and capital market, 160; government and prices, 93; and market mechanism, 31; price structure, 99; role of government, 49; subsidy, 53, 54
cost: structure, 22
Cotton Fund, 96
construction, 67, 79; Gaza and West Bank, 164
Councils on Business Restrictions, 95
credit: allocation, 102
currency, 68; devaluation, 95; devaluation strategy, 132

defense, 67, 134; economic policy, 81–84; expenditures, 83; policy for West Bank and Gaza Strip, 169
demand: and balanced budget, 131; elasticity, 79; inflation, 125
Denmark, 117, 146
distribution, 12; products and consumers, 13

economic efficiency, 102; application, 64; concept, 60; decentralization, 45; defined, 3–9; government enterprise, 151; income distribution, 146; marginal substitutabilities, 12; monopoly, 54; planning and price mechanism, 155; price mechanism, 41; small firms, 47
education, 53, 75
employment: Arabs, 135
employment, 69, 164; Arabs, 135; increase, 74; inflation, 128; lack of, 82; price stability, 38; wage level and labor, 112, 113
equalization funds, 88
exports, 61; increase, 80; premiums, 86; premiums and exchange rate, 86

*185*